content

SWEATER & HAT set

Sweater

SIZES
Sized for 6, 12, 18, 24 months. Shown in size 12 months.

MEASUREMENTS
Chest 19 (21, 22, 23)"/48 (53.5, 56, 58.5)cm
Length 10 (10½, 11¼, 11¾)"/25.5 (26.5, 28.5, 30)cm
Upper arm 8 (8½, 9, 9½)"/20.5 (21.5, 23, 24)cm

GAUGE
18 sts and 24 rows to 4"/10cm over St st using size 7 (4.5mm) needles.
Take time to check your gauge.

K1, P1 RIB
(over any number of sts)
Row 1 (RS) *K1, p1; rep from * to end.
Row 2 K the knit sts and p the purl sts.
Rep row 2 for k1, p1 rib.

STRIPE PATTERN
Work 4 rows MC, 4 rows CC, 2 rows MC, 2 rows CC, 4 rows MC, 2 rows CC, work in MC to end.

BACK
With MC, cast on 43 (47, 49, 51) sts. Work in k1, p1 rib for 4 rows. Work in St st (k on RS, p on WS) until piece measures 5¼ (5¾, 5¾, 6¼)"/13.5 (14.5, 14.5, 16)cm from beg, end with a WS row. With CC, work 2 rows.

Beg stripe pat and shape raglan armhole
Working in stripe pat, bind off 2 sts at beg of next 2 rows—39 (43, 45, 47) sts. Work 0 (0, 2, 2) rows even.
Next (dec) row (RS) K1, SKP, k to last 3 sts, k2tog, k1—2 sts dec'd.

MATERIALS
Yarn (4)
• 3½oz/100g, 220yd/210m each of any worsted weight wool and acrylic blend yarn in beige (MC) and blue (CC)
Needles
• One pair size 7 (4.5mm) needles *or size to obtain gauge*
• One size 7 (4.5mm) circular needle, 12"/30cm long *or size to obtain gauge*

Next row (WS) Purl.
Rep last 2 rows 8 (8, 9, 9) times more—21 (25, 25, 27) sts.
Next (dec) row (RS) K1, SKP, k4, bind off center 7 (11, 11, 13) sts, k4, k2tog, k1. Working both sides at once, bind off 3 sts at each neck edge once, bind off rem 3 sts each side.

FRONT
Work same as for back.

SLEEVES
With MC, cast on 26 (28, 31, 33) sts. Work in k1, p1 rib for 4 rows. Work in St st and inc 1 st each side every 4th (6th, 6th, 6th) row 2 (3, 2, 1) times, then every 6th (8th, 8th, 8th) row 3 (2, 3, 4) times—36 (38, 41, 43) sts. Work even until piece measures 5¾ (6¾, 7¼, 7¾)"/14.5 (17, 18.5, 19.5)cm. With CC, work 2 rows.

Beg stripe pat and shape raglan cap
Working in stripe pat, bind off 2 sts at beg of next 2 rows.
Dec row 1 (RS) K1, SKP, SKP, k to last 5 sts, k2tog, k2tog, k1—4 sts dec.
Next row (WS) Purl.
Rep last 2 rows 1 (1, 0, 0) times more.
Dec row 2 (RS) K1, SKP, k to last 3 sts, k2tog, k1—2 sts dec.

Next row (WS) Purl.
Rep last 2 rows 7 (7, 10, 10) times more—8 (10, 11, 13) sts. Bind off.

FINISHING
Sew raglan sleeves into raglan armholes. Sew side and sleeve seams.

COLLAR
With circular needle and MC, pick up and k 17 (20, 20, 22) sts from back neck edge, 7 (9, 10, 11) sts from top of left sleeve, 17 (20, 20, 22) sts from front neck edge, 7 (9, 10, 11) sts from top of right sleeve—48 (58, 60, 66) sts. Join and place marker for beg of rnd. Work in k1, p1 rib for 4 rnds. Bind off loosely in rib.

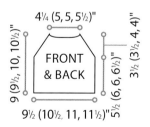

4¼ (5, 5, 5½)"
9 (9½, 10, 10½)"
FRONT & BACK
3½ (3½, 4, 4)"
5½ (6, 6½)"
9½ (10½, 11, 11½)"

8 (8½, 9, 9½)"
SLEEVE
3½ (3½, 4, 4)"
6 (7, 7½, 8)"
5¾ (6, 6¾, 7¼)"

Hat

SIZES
Sized for Baby, Toddler, and Child. Shown in size Baby.

MEASUREMENTS
Head circumference 13½ (17, 18½)"/34.5 (43, 47)cm
Length 6 (7, 7½)"/15 (18, 19)cm

GAUGE
18 sts and 24 rnds to 4"/10cm over St st using size 7 (4.5mm) needles.
Take time to check your gauge.

K1, P1 RIB
(over an even number of sts)
Rnd 1 *K1, p1; rep from * around.
Rep rnd 1 for k1, p1 rib.

HAT
With circular needle and MC, cast on 60 (76, 84) sts. Place marker for beg of rnd and join, taking care not to twist sts. Work in k1, p1 rib until piece measures 1"/2.5cm from beg.

MATERIALS
Yarn (4)
Any worsted weight wool and acrylic blend yarn
- 3½oz/100g, 220yd/210m in beige (MC)
- Small amount in blue (CC)

Needles
- One size 7 (4.5mm) circular needle, 12"/30cm long *or size to obtain gauge*
- One set (5) size 7 (4.5mm) double-pointed needles (dpns)

Notions
- Stitch marker

Beg stripe sequence
Rnds 1–2 With MC, knit.
Rnds 3–6 With CC, knit.
Rnds 7–8 With MC, knit.
Rnds 9–10 With CC, knit.
Cont in St st (k every rnd) with MC only until piece measures 4 (4¼, 4½)"/10 (11, 11.5)cm from beg.

Shape crown
Change to dpns, dividing sts evenly over 4 dpns—15 (19, 21) sts on each needle.
Dec rnd [K to last 2 sts on needle, k2tog] 4 times—4 sts dec'd.
Rep dec rnd every rnd 12 (16, 18) times more—2 sts on each dpn, 8 sts in rnd.
Cut yarn, leaving long tail. Thread yarn through rem sts and pull tight to close. ▪

EARLY bloomer

SIZES
Sized for 3–6, 9, 12, 18 months. Shown in size 18 months.

MEASUREMENTS
Chest 20 (22, 24, 26)"/51 (56, 61, 66)cm
Length 11 (12, 13½, 14½)"/28 (30.5, 34, 37)cm
Upper arm 9 (10, 11, 12)"/23 (25.5, 28, 30.5)cm

GAUGE
22 sts and 40 rows to 4"/10cm over St st using size 6 (4mm) needles.
Take time to check your gauge.

NOTE
This pattern is for a knitter who has experience with crochet. The delicate collar, buttons and hat applique are crocheted.

SEED STITCH
(over an even number of sts)
Row 1 *K1, p1; rep from* to end.
Row 2 K the purl sts and p the knit sts.
Rep row 2 for seed st.

STITCH GLOSSARY
Sl-s dec (left-slanting dec, worked on RS)
With right needle behind left needle, insert right needle through back loops of next 2 sts on left needle. K these 2 sts tog.

Sl-s dec (left-slanting dec, worked on WS)
With right needle behind left needle, insert right needle into back loop of second st and then into back loop of first st on left needle which twists 2 sts, purl these 2 sts tog.

MATERIALS
Yarn ③
Any DK weight cotton yarn
• 8¾oz/250g, 680yd/620m (8¾oz/250g, 680yd/620m; 10½oz/300g, 820yd/750m; 10½oz/300g, 820yd/750m) in white (MC)
• 1¾oz/50g, 140yd/120m in pink (CC)

Needles
• One pair size 6 (4mm) needles *or size to obtain gauge*

Notions
• Size 5 (1.75mm) steel crochet hook
• Stitch holder
• 5¾"/14.5cm plastic rings

Sdv dec (double vertical dec, worked on RS)
Insert right needle into next 2 sts on left needle as if you were knitting them tog and slip them to right needle, k next st on left needle, with left needle, pull both slipped sts over knit st.

Sdv dec (double vertical dec, worked on WS).
Insert right needle into next 2 sts on left needle one by one as if you were knitting them, slip them to right needle. (2 twisted sts on right needle), sl 2 slipped sts to left needle, keeping them twisted, insert right needle through back loops of second and first slipped sts and sl them tog off left needle. P next st. With left needle, pass 2 slipped sts over purl st and off right needle.

Sr-s dec (right-slanting dec, worked on RS)
Knit one st, slip one st knitwise; return slipped st and knit st to left needle. Pass slipped st over knit st and off left needle; return completed st back to right needle.

Sr-s dec (right-slanting dec, worked on WS)
Slip next st on the left needle purlwise, then purl one st. With left needle, pass the slipped st over the purl st and off the right needle.

Dec 1 sc
Draw up one loop in next 2 sts then draw yarn through all 3 lps on needle.

Sweater
BACK
With MC, cast on 56 (60, 66, 72) sts. Work in seed st for 10¼ (11¼, 12¾, 13¾)"/ 26 (28.5, 32.5, 35) cm from beg. Bind off.

POCKET LINING
(make 2)
With MC, cast on 16 (16, 17, 17) sts. Work in St st for 2 (2½, 2½, 2½)"/5 (5, 6.5, 6.5)cm, end with a WS row. Place sts on a holder.

EARLY bloomer

LEFT FRONT
With MC, cast on 28 (30, 33, 36) sts. Work in seed st for 26 (26, 28, 30) rows, end with a WS row.
Next row (RS) Cont in pat, work first 6 (7, 8, 9) sts, bind off next 16 (16, 17, 18) sts, work to end.
Next row (WS) Work 6 (7, 8, 9) sts, work sts from one lining holder, work to end. Cont in pat until piece measures 8¼ (9½, 10¾, 11¾)"/21 (24, 27.5, 30)cm from beg, end with a RS row.

Shape neck
Next row (WS) Bind off first 4 (4, 5, 5) sts, work to end. Cont to shape neck by binding off from neck edge 3 sts once, then 2 sts once. Dec 1 st at neck edge 4 times—15 (17, 19, 22) sts. Work even until piece measures same as back. Bind off all sts.

RIGHT FRONT
Work as for left front reversing all shaping.

SLEEVES
With MC, cast on 36 (36, 40, 40) sts. Work in seed st and AT SAME TIME, inc 1 st each side every 6th row 0 (10, 11, 13) times and every 8th row 7 (0, 0, 0) times—50 (56, 62, 66) sts. Work even in pat until piece measures 6 (6½, 7¼, 8)"/15 (16.5, 18.5, 20.5)cm from beg. Bind off all sts.

FINISHING
Block pieces to measurements. Sew pocket linings in place. Sew shoulder seams. Mark 4½ (5, 5½, 6)"/11 (13, 14, 15)cm down from shoulders for armholes. Sew sleeves between markers. Sew side and sleeve seams.

Sleeve border
With crochet hook and RS facing, join MC with a sl st at seam. Work 4 rnds of sc. Fasten off.

Pocket border
With crochet hook and WS facing, join MC with sl st at left end pocket opening, ch 1, sc across—16 (16, 17, 18) sts. Turn. Work 3 more rows sc. Fasten off. Sew ends of pocket border to front.

Body border
With crochet hook and RS facing, join MC with sl st in lower left front corner, ch 1.
Rnd 1 Working evenly across edges and working 3 sc in corners and at beg of neck edges, sc around, join with a sl st. On left front, mark for 5 buttonholes: first one between 2nd and 3rd sts down from corner st, last one between 2nd and 3rd up from corner st and 3 more evenly spaced between.
Rnd 2 Continuing to work 3 sts into corner sts, sc around and (ch 4, sk 4) sts over each marker, join.

Rnd 3 Work around as established, working 4 sc in each ch-4 sp, join. Rep rnd 1 once more, dec 4 sc evenly spaced along neck edge. Fasten off.

BUTTONS
With MC and crochet hook, ch 5 loosely, join with a sl st to form a chain ring. Place plastic ring over yarn ring, with loop at front and yarn behind. Ch 1 and work 10 sc into center of both rings covering plastic ring and yarn ring, join with a sl st. Leaving a tail, fasten off.

COLLAR
With WS facing, using CC and crochet hook, join with a sl st about ½"/1.5cm from neck edge.
Row 1 Ch 3 (counts as 1 dc and 1 ch). *sk 1 sc, dc in next sc, dc in next sc, ch 1; rep from *, end with sk 1 sc, dc in next sc and at ½"/1.5cm from right neck corner, turn.
Row 2 Ch 2 (counts as 1 dc), dc 2 more in 1 ch-sp, *ch 1, 3 dc in next ch-sp; rep from *, turn.
Row 3 Ch 2 (counts as 1 dc and 1 ch), sk 2, *dc 3 in next ch-1 sp, ch 2, sk 3; rep from *, end 3 dc, ch 1, sk last 2 sts, dc 1 in 2nd ch of ch 2 in previous row. Fasten off.

Picot edge
With crochet hook and RS of collar facing, beg at left side, join CC with a sl st,*sc 3, ch 3, sc into first ch of 3 ch (picot made); rep from * along edges of collar. Fasten off.

Hat
With MC, cast on 66 (71, 76, 81) sts. Work in St st for 1"/2.5cm. Cont in seed st until piece measures 4 (4½, 5, 5½)"/10 (11.5, 12.5, 14)cm from beg

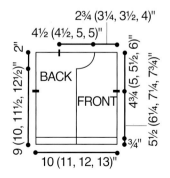

(with edge rolled), end with a WS row.

Next row (RS) Cont in pat, sl-s dec, *work next 10 (11, 12, 13) sts, sdv dec; rep from * 3 times more, work next 10 (11, 12, 13) sts sr-s dec.

Next row (WS) Sl-s dec, *work next 8 (9, 10, 11) sts, sdv dec; rep from * 3 times more. Work next 8 (9, 10, 11) sts, sr-s dec. Working 2 sts less between decs on every row, cont dec over decs of previous row until there is 0 (1, 0, 1) st left between decs.

Leaving a long tail, pull yarn through rem 8 (13, 8, 13) sts. Sew seams with mattress st (inserting into center of first dec line at both edge of work) to create the 5th line.

Flower
With crochet hook and CC, ch 5, join with a sl st to form a ring.

Rnd 1 Ch1, work 10 sc into center of ring, join with a sl st.

Rnd 2 Ch 1, * sc in next st, (dc, tr, dc) in next st; rep from * around, join with a sl st. Leave a tail and fasten off.

Leaf
(Work in rounds and half rnds)
With crochet hook and CC, ch 7.

Rnd 1 Insert hook into 2nd ch from hook and tr, sc 5, work 3 sc into last ch then working 5 sc into each ch along lower side of beg ch, work 3 sc into last ch of beg ch.

Rnd 2 Sc into next 4 sts, ch 2, turn.

Rnd 3 Sc into next 5 sts, sc 3 into corner st, sc into next 5 sts, ch 2, turn.

Rnd 4 Sc into next 6 sts, sl st into next st, ch 2. Leaving a tail, fasten off.

FINISHING
Sew on buttons and appliqués. ■

STRIPED
pullovers

SIZES
Sized for 3–6, 6–9, 9–12, 12–18, 18–24 months. Shown in size 3–6 months.

MEASUREMENTS
Chest 19½ (21½, 23, 25, 27)"/49.5 (54.5, 58.5, 63.5, 68.5)cm
Length 10 (10¾, 12, 13, 14¼)"/25.5 (27.5, 30.5, 33, 36)cm
Upper arm 7¾ (8¼, 9, 9½, 10½)"/19.5 (21, 23, 24, 26.5)cm

GAUGE
27 sts and 32 rows to 4"/10cm over St st and stripe pattern using size 4 (3.5mm) needles.
Take time to check your gauge.

STRIPE PATTERN
Beg with a RS row, work in St st (k on RS, p on WS) as foll: [2 rows CC, 2 rows MC] 3 times, 2 rows MC. Rep these 14 rows for stripe pat.

BACK
With size 2 (2.75mm) needles and MC, cast on 66 (72, 78, 84, 90) sts. Work in garter st (k every row) for ¾"/1.5cm, end with a RS row. Change to size 4 (3.5mm) needles.

Garter st detail
Next row (WS) K3, p to last 3 sts, k3.
Next row Knit.
Next row (WS) K3, p to last 3 sts, k3.

Beg stripe pat
Next row (RS) With CC, knit.
Cont in St st over all sts until 14-row stripe pat has been worked 3 times. Cont in MC only until piece measures 6¼ (6¾, 7½, 8¼, 9)"/16 (17, 19, 21, 23) cm from beg, end with a WS row.

MATERIALS
Yarn ❷
Boy's version
Any sport weight cotton yarn
• 3½oz/100g, 280yd/260m (3½oz/100g, 280yd/260m; 5¼oz/150g, 420yd/390m; 5¼oz/150g, 420yd/390m; 7oz/200g, 550yd/510m) in light blue (MC)
• 1¾oz/50g, 140yd/130m (1¾oz/50g, 140yd/130m; 3½oz/100g, 280yd/260m; 3½oz/100g, 280yd/260m; 3½oz/100g, 280yd/260m) in light green (CC)

Girl's version
Any sport weight cotton yarn
• 3½oz/100g, 280yd/260m (3½oz/100g, 280yd/260m; 5¼oz/150g, 420yd/390m; 5¼oz/150g, 420yd/390m; 7oz/200g, 550yd/510m) in coral (MC)
• 1¾oz/50g, 140yd/130m (1¾oz/50g, 140yd/130m; 3½oz/100g, 280yd/260m; 3½oz/100g, 280yd/260m; 3½oz/100g, 280yd/260m) in light pink (CC)

For both
• One pair size 4 (3.5mm) needles *or size to obtain gauge*
• One pair each sizes 2 and 3 (2.75 and 3.25mm) needles
• One size 2 (2.75mm) circular needle, 24"/60cm long
• Two ½"/12mm buttons
• Stitch holder

Shape armholes
Bind off 4 sts at beg of next 2 rows—58 (64, 70, 76, 82) sts. Work even in MC until back measures 9¼ (10, 11½, 12¼, 13½)"/23.5 (25.5, 28.5, 31.5, 34)cm from beg, end with a WS row.

Divide for neck
Work 14 (17, 19, 22, 24) sts for right neck, sl rem sts to holder. Work right neck in St st for ¾"/2cm, end with a WS row. Bind off right neck. Sl last 14 (17, 19, 22, 24) sts of row from holder to size 4 (3.5mm) needles for left neck, leaving 30 (30, 32, 32, 34) center sts on holder. Work even in St st until left neck measures ¾"/2cm, end with a WS row.

Buttonband
Change to size 3 (3.25mm) needles, knit 3 rows. Bind off on WS, cut yarn.

Back neckband
With RS facing, circular needle and MC from right neck, pick up and k 7 sts along right neck edge, place marker (pm), k30 (30, 32, 32, 34) sts from holder, pm, pick up and k 9 sts along left neck edge to end—46 (46, 48, 48, 50) sts. Sl markers (sm) every row. Knit 1 WS row.
Next (dec) row (RS) [K to 2 sts before marker, ssk, sm, k2tog] twice, k to end—42 (42, 44, 44, 46) sts. Knit 1 row. Rep last 2 rows once more—38 (38, 40, 40, 42) sts.
Next row (RS) [Bind off to 2 sts before marker, ssk, bind off over ssk, remove marker, k2tog, bind off ssk over k2tog, bind off k2tog] twice, bind off to end.

FRONT
Work same as back until front measures 8¼ (9, 10¼, 11¼, 12½)"/21 (23, 26, 28.5, 32)cm from beg, end with a WS row—58 (64, 70, 76, 82) sts.

Divide for neck
Work 14 (17, 19, 22, 24) sts for left neck, sl rem sts to st holder. Work left neck in St st for 1¾"/4.5cm, end with a WS row.

THE TALE OF
BENJAMIN BUNNY

BEATRIX POTTER
The original and authorized edition

STRIPED pullovers

Buttonhole band
Change to size 3 (3.25mm) needles, knit 2 rows.
Next (buttonhole) row (RS) K8 (10, 12, 14, 16) sts, yo, k2tog, k to end.
Knit 2 rows. Bind off.

Right neck
Sl last 14 (17, 19, 22, 24) sts from st holder to size 4 (3.5mm) needles for right neck, leaving 30 (30, 32, 32, 34) sts center sts on holder. Work even in St st until armhole measures same length as right back armhole. Bind off.

Front neckband
With RS facing, circular needle and MC, pick up and k 13 sts along left neck edge, pm, k30 (30, 32, 32, 34) sts from st holder, pm, pick up and k 11 sts along right neck edge to end—54 (54, 56, 56, 58) sts. Knit 1 WS row.
Next (dec) row (RS) [K to 2 sts before marker, ssk, sm, k2tog] twice, k to end—50 (50, 52, 52, 54) sts. Knit 1 row.
Next (dec and buttonhole) row (RS) K1, k2tog, yo, [k to 2 sts before marker, ssk, sm, k2tog] twice, k to end—46 (46, 48, 48, 50) sts. Knit 1 row. Bind off as for back neckband.

SLEEVES
With size 3 (3.25mm) needles and MC, cast on 42 (46, 46, 50, 54) sts.

Beg ribbing
Next row (RS) K2, [p2, k2] to end.
Next row (WS) K the knit sts and p the purl sts.
Rep last 2 rows for k2, p2 rib until piece measures 1"/2.5cm from beg. Change to size 4 (3.5mm) needles.
Next row (RS) Knit.
Next row Purl.

Shape sleeve
Next (inc) row (RS) K3, M1, k to last 3 sts, M1, k3—44 (48, 48, 52, 56) sts.
Next row Purl.

Beg stripe pat
Next row (RS) With CC, knit.
Cont in St st and stripe pat, and rep inc row every 6th row 4 (4, 6, 6, 7) times more—52 (56, 60, 64, 70) sts.
When 14-row stripe pat has been worked 3 times, cont in MC only until piece measures 6¼ (6¾, 7½, 8¼, 9½)"/16 (17, 19, 21, 24)cm from beg, end with a WS row. Bind off.

FINISHING
Lightly block pieces to measurements. Sew right shoulder/neckband seam. Place buttonhole band over button band and tack in place at armhole edge. Sew sleeves into armholes, working through both layers of button bands on left sleeve. Sew sleeve seams. Sew side seams, ending at top of garter st detail. Sew buttons opposite buttonholes. ■

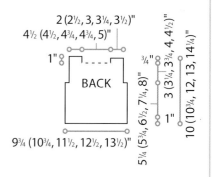

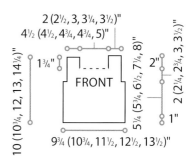

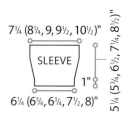

SIZES
Cardigan sized for 6, 12, 18 months. Shown in size 6 months; Hat & Blanket in one size only.

MEASUREMENTS
Cardigan
Chest 23 (24, 25)"/58.5 (61, 63.5)cm
Length 10½ (11, 12)"/26.5 (28, 30.5)cm
Upper arm 10 (10½, 11)"/25.5 (26.5, 28)cm

Hat
Circumference 16"/40.5cm

Blanket
Approximately 28 x 34"/71 x 86cm

GAUGE
20 sts and 26 rows to 4"/10cm over St st using larger needles and DK weight cotton yarn.
Take time to check your gauge.

K1, P1 RIB
(over any number of sts)
Row 1 (RS) *K1, p1; rep from * to end.
Row 2 K the knit sts and p the purl sts.
Rep row 2 for k1, p1 rib.

NOTE
Use a separate bobbin for each color section when working charts. Do not carry yarn across back of work.

STRIPE PATTERN
*2 rows A, 2 rows B; rep from * for stripe pat.

Blanket

Note Work blanket in St st with 5-st garter borders in B on each side.

MATERIALS
Yarn ③ ④
Blanket
Any DK weight cotton yarn
• 7oz/200g, 440yd/410m in pink (A)
• 9¾oz/250g, 540yd/500m in white (B)
Any worsted weight angora and wool blend yarn
• 1oz/25g, 110yd/110m in white (C)

Cardigan & Hat
Any DK weight cotton yarn
• 5¼oz/150g, 330yd/310m (7oz/200g, 440yd/410m; 7oz/200g, 440yd/410m) in pink (A)
• 3½oz/100g, 220yd/210m (5¼oz/150g, 330yd/310m; 7oz/200g, 440yd/410m) in white (B)
Any worsted weight angora and wool blend yarn
• 1oz/25g, 110yd/110m in white (C)

Needles
• One pair each sizes 4 and 6 (3.5 and 4mm) needles *or size to obtain gauge*

Notions
• Embroidery thread in blue (D)
• Crochet hook size G/6 (4mm)
• Four ½"/13mm white ball shank buttons

With B, cast on 144 sts. Work in garter st (k every row) for 8 rows.
Next row Work 5 sts in garter st with B, work in St st and stripe pattern to last 5 sts, join 2nd ball of B and work 5 sts in garter st. Cont as established until piece measures 29"/73.5cm from beg, end with 2 rows B. Work in St st with A for 6 rows.

Beg 18-st bunny chart
Next row (RS) Work 5 st garter border with B, work 20 sts A, *work 18-st bunny chart, work 20 sts A; rep from *,

end 5 sts garter border with B.
Cont as established until 18 rows of chart are complete. Work in St st with A for 10 rows. With B, work 8 rows in garter st. Bind off.

FINISHING
Eyes
With D, form French knot as indicated on chart.

Tail
With C and crochet hook, chain 16, fasten off. Spiral into circle and attach as indicated on chart.

Ear
With C and smaller needles, cast on 3 sts.
Next (inc) row (RS) K1, M1, k to last st, M1, k1—2 sts inc'd. K 1 row.
Rep last 2 rows—7 sts.
K 12 rows.
Next (dec) row (RS) K1, ssk, k to last 3 sts, k2tog, k1—2 sts dec'd. K 1 row.
Rep last 2 rows—3 sts.
Cut yarn and pull through remaining sts, fasten off. Fold ear and attach as indicated on chart, leaving top and sides open.

BUNNY cardi, hat & blanket

Cardigan

BACK

With smaller needles and B, cast on 58 (60, 62) sts. Work in k1, p1 rib for 8 rows. Change to larger needles, and work in St st.
*Join A and work 2 rows, then work 2 rows B; rep from * once. Cont with A only until piece measures 11 (11½, 12)"/28 (29, 30)cm from beg.
Next row (WS) Bind off 17 (18, 19) sts for shoulder, p24 sts and place on holder, bind off remaining 17 (18, 19) sts for shoulder.

RIGHT FRONT

With smaller needles and B, cast on 27 (29, 31) sts. Work as for back through stripe pat, work 2 rows A.

Beg 16-st bunny chart

Next row (RS) Work 5 sts A, join C and work 16 sts of bunny chart, work 6 sts A. Cont as established until 16 rows of chart are complete.
Cont with A only until piece measures 8½ (9, 9½)"/21.5 (23, 24)cm from beg, end with a WS row.

Shape neck

Next row (RS) Bind off 4 sts (neck edge), work to end. Cont to bind off from neck edge 2 sts twice, then 1 st twice—17 (18, 19) sts. Work even until piece measures same as back. Bind off on WS.

LEFT FRONT

Work as for right front, reversing direction of bunny, chart placement, and all shaping.

SLEEVES

With smaller needles and B, cast on 32 (34, 36) sts. Work in k1, p1 rib for 8 rows. Change to larger needles, work in St st and stripe pat inc 4 sts evenly across the first row—36 (38, 40) sts.
Inc row Inc 1 st each side every 6 rows 7 times—50 (52, 54) sts.
Work even until piece measures 8 (8½, 9)"/21.5 (23, 24)cm from beg. Bind off on WS.

FINISHING

Sew shoulder seams. Mark 5 (5¼, 5½)"/12.5 (13.5, 14)cm down from shoulder at each armhole edge. Sew top of sleeve at armhole edge between markers. Sew side seams.

Neckband

With RS facing, smaller needles and B, pick up and k 62 sts evenly around neck edge. Work in k1, p1 rib for 7 rows. Bind off on WS in rib.

Right front band

With smaller needles and B, pick up and k 55 (68, 62) sts evenly along right front edge. Work in k1, p1 rib for 3 rows.
Buttonhole row (RS) Rib 4 sts, bind off *2 sts in rib, rib 13 sts; rep from * 3 times, rib 4 sts. Rib next row, casting on 2 sts over bound off sts. Work 2 rows even. Bind off in rib.

Left front band

With smaller needles and B, pick up and k 55 (58, 62) sts evenly along left front edge. Work in k1, p1 rib for 7 rows. Bind off in rib. Sew buttons opposite buttonholes. For eyes, tail, and ears see blanket instructions.

Hat

With smaller needles and B, cast on 84 sts. Work in k1, p1 rib for 7 rows. Change to larger needles, and cont in St st. Join A and work 2 rows, work 2 rows B, then 2 rows A.

Beg 14-st bunny chart

Next row (RS) Work 35 sts A, join C and work 14-st bunny chart, work 35 sts in A.
Cont as established until 13 row chart is complete. Work with A only until piece measures 4"/10cm from beg, end with a WS row.

Shape crown

Next (dec) row (RS) *K10, k2tog; rep from * to end—77 sts. P 1 row.
Next (dec) row *K9, k2tog; rep from * to end—70 sts.
Cont to dec in this manner, dec 7 sts every RS row, 5 times more. Pull yarn through rem sts. Draw up tightly and sew back seam.

FINISHING

Eye
See blanket instructions.

Tail
With crochet hook and C, chain 14, fasten off. Spiral into circle and attach as indicated on chart.

Ear
With crochet hook and C, form 14 st chain; loop and stitch centers tog. Attach as indicated on chart.

Top of hat
With crochet hook and B, form 16 st chain; spiral into circle and attach to center top. ■

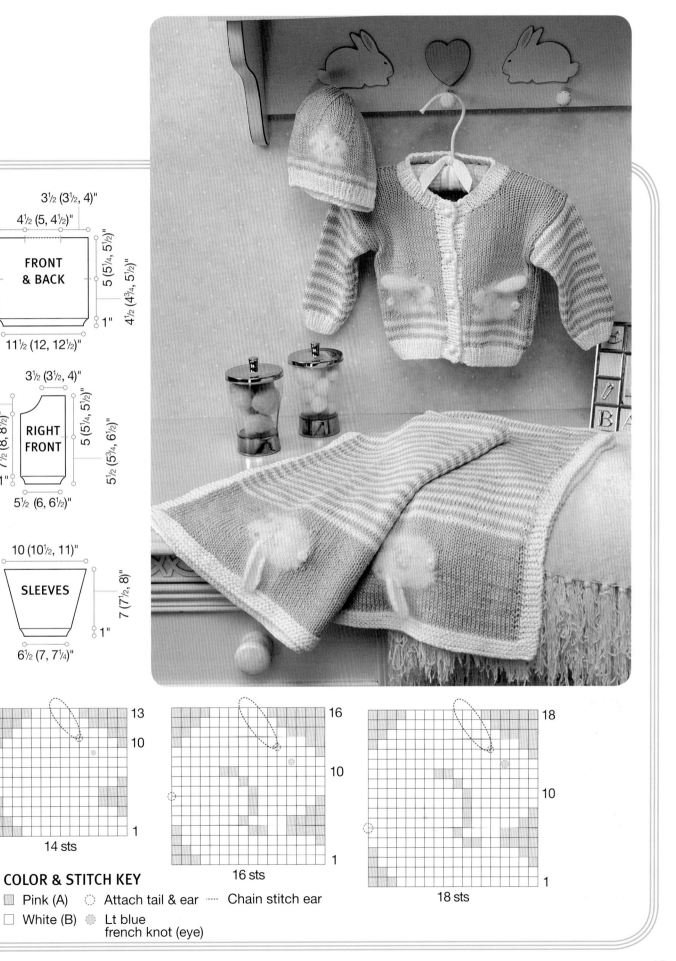

FRONT & BACK

3½ (3½, 4)"

4½ (5, 4½)"

10½ (11, 12)"

5 (5¼, 5½)"

4½ (4¾, 5½)"

1"

11½ (12, 12½)"

RIGHT FRONT

3½ (3½, 4)"

2 (2, 2½)"

5 (5¼, 5½)"

7½ (8, 8½)"

5¾ (5¾, 6½)"

1"

5½ (6, 6½)"

5½ (5¾, 6½)"

SLEEVES

10 (10½, 11)"

7 (7½, 8)"

1"

6½ (7, 7¼)"

13

10

1

14 sts

16

10

1

16 sts

18

10

1

18 sts

COLOR & STITCH KEY

▨ Pink (A)   ◌ Attach tail & ear   ⋯⋯ Chain stitch ear

☐ White (B)   ⬤ Lt blue french knot (eye)

13

GARTER STITCH
layette

SIZES
Sized for Newborn–3 months, 6–9, 12–18 months. Shown in size 6–9 months.

MEASUREMENTS
Sweater
Chest (buttoned) 19 (21, 23)"/48 (53.5, 58.5)cm
Length 9½ (10, 12)"/24 (25.5, 30.5)cm
Upper arm 4½ (5, 5½)"/11.5 (12.5, 14)cm

Blanket
Approximately 24 x 27"/61 x 68cm

Hat
Circumference 13½ (16, 18½)"/34 (40.5, 47.5)cm

Booties
Length (foot) 3½"/9cm
Foot circumference 5½"/14cm

GAUGE
18 sts and 36 rows = 4"/10cm over garter stitch using size 8 (5mm) needles.
Take time to check your gauge.

Sweater
BACK
With straight needles and A, cast on 42 (48, 52) sts. Beg with a RS row, work in garter st (k every row) for 9½ (10, 12)"/24 (25.5, 30.5)cm, end with a WS row.
Next row (RS) K13 (15, 16) and place on a holder, bind off next 16 (18, 20) sts for back neck, k to end and place on 2nd holder.

LEFT FRONT
With straight needles and A, cast on 16 (18, 20) sts.

MATERIALS
Yarn (4)
Any worsted weight wool yarn
• 8¾oz/250g, 390yd/360m (10½oz/300g, 470yd/430m; 14oz/400g, 620yd/570m) in dark purple (A)
• 17½oz/500g, 770yd/710m in light purple (B)

Needles
• One pair size 8 (5mm) needles *or size to obtain gauge*
• One size 8 (5mm) circular needle, 24"/60cm long
• One set (3) size 8 (5mm) double-pointed needles (dpns)

Notions
• 3 Stitch holders
• Stitch markers

Shape curve
Next (inc) row (RS) K to last 4 sts, inc in next 3 sts, k1—19 (21, 23) sts.
K 3 rows even.
Next (inc) row K to last 3 sts, inc in next 2 sts, k1—21 (23, 25) sts. Rep last 4 rows once more—23 (25, 27) sts.
K 5 rows even.
Next row K to last 2 sts, inc in next st, k1—24 (26, 28 sts).
Rep last 6 rows once more—25 (27, 29) sts. Cont even in garter st until piece measures 8 (8½, 10½)"/20.5 (21.5, 26.5) cm from beg, end with a RS row.

Shape neck
Next row (WS) Bind off 7 (7, 8) sts, k to end.
Cont to bind off from neck edge 2 sts twice, k2tog at neck edge once—13 (15, 16) sts.
Work even until piece measures same as back. Place sts on a holder. Place markers for 4 buttons, with first marker

½"/1.5cm down from neck edge, last marker ½"/1.5cm up from top of curve, and the other 2 markers spaced evenly between.

RIGHT FRONT
With straight needles and A, cast on 16 (18, 20) sts.

Shape curve
Next (inc) row (RS) K1, inc in next 3 sts, k to end—19 (21, 23) sts.
K 3 rows even.
Next (inc) row K1, inc in next 2 sts, k to end—21 (23, 25) sts. Rep last 4 rows once more—23 (25, 27) sts.
K 5 rows even.
Next (inc) row K1, inc in next st, k to end—24 (26, 28) sts.
Rep last 6 rows once more—25 (27, 29) sts. Cont as for left front, working neck shaping on RS rows and working final dec at neck edge as ssp, and AT THE SAME TIME, work buttonholes opposite markers as foll: K2, yo, k2tog, k to end. Place sts on a holder.

Shoulder seams
With WS facing each other, and front of garment facing you, place sts of back and front left shoulders on two parallel dpns. Seam will be visible on RS of garment. Work 3-needle bind off (refer to page 16). Rep for right shoulder.

SLEEVES
Place markers on front and back 4½ (5, 5½)"/11.5 (12.5, 14)cm down from shoulder seams. With RS facing, straight needles and A, pick up and k 40 (45, 49) sts evenly between markers. Working in garter st, dec 1 st each edge every 4th row 5 (2, 1) times, every 6th row 4 (7, 0) times, every 8th row 0 (0, 7) times—22 (27, 33) sts, end with a RS row.

GARTER STITCH
layette

Cuff

Change to B, p next row for turning ridge. Cont in garter st for 2"/5cm. Bind off.

FINISHING

Sew side and sleeve seams, reversing sleeve seams at cuffs. Fold cuffs to outside.

I-cord buttons (make 4)

With 2 dpns and A, cast on 3 sts. *K 1 row. Without turning work, slide the sts back to opposite end of needle to work next row from RS. Pull yarn tightly from the end of the row. Rep from * until I-cord measures approx 4"/10cm. Do not bind off. Tie I-cord in knot a little above cast-on edge. Cut yarn, leaving a short end for sewing. Unravel loose sts to just above knot. Thread cut end into yarn needle and slip it through these 3 open sts. Draw yarn through to gather sts. Insert needle into cast-on edge and sew ends tog. Sew buttons to right front opposite buttonholes.

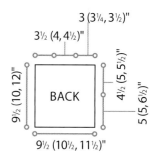

3 (3¼, 3½)"
3½ (4, 4½)"
9½ (10, 12)"
BACK
4½ (5, 5½)"
5 (5, 6½)"
9½ (10½, 11½)"

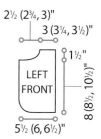

2½ (2¾, 3)"
3 (3¼, 3½)"
1½"
LEFT FRONT
8 (8½, 10½)"
5½ (6, 6½)"

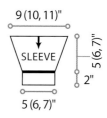

9 (10, 11)"
SLEEVE
5 (6, 7)"
2"
5 (6, 7)"

THE THREE-NEEDLE BIND-OFF

1 Place the shoulder sts of the front and back together, with the needles parallel, as shown.

2 Insert a 3rd needle into the first sts on front and back needles and k these 2 sts tog—I st on RH needle.

3 K the next 2 sts tog from front and back needles, then pass 2nd st over the first to bind off.

4 Repeat step 3 until all sts have been bound off. A decorative ridge will show on the right side.

Blanket

With circular needle and B, cast on 108 sts. Work in garter st for 2 rows.
Next (eyelet) row K2, yo, k2tog, k to last 4 sts, k2tog, yo, k2. Work even in garter st until blanket measures 26½"/67cm. Rep eyelet row. K 2 more rows. Bind off.

FINISHING
I-cord ties (make 4)
With 2 dpns and A, cast on 4 sts. Work I-cord as for buttons for 12"/30.5cm. Bind off. Thread I-cord through eyelets, knot around corner of blanket, then tie cord in a bow.

Hat

CUFFED BRIM
With straight needles and A, cast on 60 (72, 84) sts. Beg with a RS row, work in garter st for 2"/5cm, end with a WS row. P next row for turning ridge.

BODY
Change to B and cont in garter st for 3½"/9cm, end with a WS row.

Shape crown
Next (dec) row (RS) *Place marker (pm), k2tog, k3 (4, 5); rep from * to end—48 (60, 72) sts. Work 3 rows even.
Next (dec) row (RS) *K2tog, work to next marker; rep from * to end—36 (48, 60) sts.
Rep last 4 rows 1 (2, 3) times more—24 sts. Work 1 row even.
Next row K2tog across—12 sts. Work 1 row even.
Rep last 2 rows once more—6 sts.
Next row [K2tog, k1] twice—4 sts. Cut yarn and place sts on a dpn.

FINISHING
With A, work I-cord as for blanket for 3"/7.5 cm. Bind off sts. Tie a knot in I-cord at top of hat. Sew back seam of hat, reversing seam at cuff. Fold cuff to outside.

Booties

With straight needles and A, cast on 8 sts. Work in garter st until piece measures 3¼"/8cm from beg. Cast on 16 sts at beg of next 2 rows—40 sts.
Work even for 11 rows. Cut yarn. Place first and last 16 sts on holders. Rejoin yarn to RS and work center 8 sts as foll: *K7, sl 1, k1 st from holder, psso, turn; rep from * until 9 sts rem on each holder. Cut yarn. Rejoin yarn to RS, k9 from first holder, k8 center sts, k9 from 2nd holder—26 sts.
Work even in garter st for 14 rows. Bind off. Sew sides of bootie to sole and sew back seam.

FINISHING
I-cord ties
With 2 dpns and B cast on 3 sts. Make two I-cord ties each 18"/45.5cm long working I-cord as for buttons. Sew center of I-cord to back seam of bootie at ankle. ■

MAKING THE BUTTONS

1 Make an I-cord piece approximately 4"/10cm long. Tie I-cord in a knot a little above the cast-on edge.

2 Cut the yarn, leaving a short end for sewing. Unravel the loose sts to just above the knot.

3 Thread the cut end into a yarn needle and slip it through these 3 open sts.

4 Draw the yarn through to gather sts. Insert needle into cast-on edge and sew ends tog.

GIRL'S LACE layette

Sweater

SIZES
Sized for Newborn–3 months, 6–9, 12–18 months. Shown in 6–9 months.

MEASUREMENTS
Chest (closed) 19¼ (22, 24½)"/49 (56, 62)cm
Length 9½ (10½, 12)"/24 (27, 30.5)cm
Upper arm 8 (9, 10)"/20.5 (23, 25.5)cm

GAUGE
24 sts and 35 rows to 4"/10cm over St st using size 5 (3.75mm) needles.
Take time to check your gauge.

NOTE
Foll the chart or written instructions below for eyelet pat.

EYELET PATTERN
(multiple of 8 sts)
Row 1 (RS) Knit.
Row 2 and all WS rows Purl.
Row 3 K1, *k2, yo, ssk, k4; rep from *, end last rep k3.
Row 5 K1, *k2tog, yo, k1, yo, ssk, k3; rep from *, end last rep k2.
Row 7 Rep row 3.
Row 9 Knit.
Row 11 K1, *k6, yo, ssk; rep from * to last 7 sts, k7.
Row 13 K2, *k3, k2tog, yo, k1, yo, ssk; rep from * to last 6 sts, k6.
Row 15 Rep row 11.
Row 16 Rep row 2.
Rep rows 1–16 for eyelet pat.

BACK
Cast on 56 (64, 72) sts. Work rows 1–16 of eyelet pat once, then work rows 1–8 once more.
Work in St st over all sts until piece

MATERIALS
Yarn [2]
• 5¼oz/150g, 420yd/390m (5¼oz/150g, 420yd/390m; 7oz/200g, 550yd/510m) of any sport weight wool yarn in coral
Needles
• One pair size 5 (3.75mm) needles *or size to obtain gauge*
Notions
• Size F/5 (3.75mm) crochet hook
• Stitch markers

measures 5 (5½, 6½)"/12.5 (14, 16.5)cm from beg. Place marker (pm) each side of next row for beg of armholes. Work even until armhole measures 4 (4½, 5)"/10 (11.5, 12.5)cm. Bind off.

LEFT FRONT
Cast on 28 (34, 36) sts.

Beg eyelet pat
Row 1 K2 (0, 2), pm, work eyelet pat over 24 (32, 32) sts, pm, k2.
Cont in pat as established, working sts each side of eyelet sts in St st, until 24 rows of pat have been worked. Work in St st over all sts until piece measures 5 (5½, 6½)"/12.5 (14, 16.5)cm from beg. Pm at beg of next RS row for armhole. Work even until piece measures 7½ (8½, 10)"/18.5 (21.5, 25)cm from beg, end with a RS row.

Shape neck
Next row (WS) Bind off 5 (6, 6) sts (neck edge), work to end. Cont to bind off from neck edge 2 (3, 3) sts once, then dec 1 st every other row 3 (4, 3) times. Work even on 18 (21, 24) sts until same length as back. Bind off sts for shoulder.

RIGHT FRONT
Work to correspond to left front, reversing shaping, placing armhole marker at end of RS row and beg eyelet pat as foll:

Row 1 (RS) K2, pm, work eyelet pat over 24 (32, 32) sts, pm, k2 (0, 2).

SLEEVES
Cast on 32 (32, 40) sts. Work in eyelet pat for 24 rows. Work in St st over all sts, inc 1 st each side on next row, then every 2nd row 2 (6, 0) times more, every 4th row 5 (4, 9) times—48 (54, 60) sts.
Work even until piece measures 6½ (7, 8)"/16.5 (17.5, 20.5)cm from beg. Bind off.

FINISHING
Block pieces to measurements. Sew shoulder seams. With center of bound-off sts at shoulder seam, sew top of sleeve to front and back above armhole markers. Sew side and sleeve seams.

Shell st border for body
With RS facing and crochet hook, join yarn at right front side seam.
Rnd 1 Ch 1, work 30 (35, 40) sc along lower edge of right front, work 3 sc in corner (mark center sc), work 29 (34, 39) sc along straight right front edge, work 3 sc in corner of neck (mark center sc), work 42 (47, 52) sc along right front neck, back neck and left front neck edge, work 3 sc in corner of neck (mark center sc), work 29 (34, 39) sc along straight left front edge, work 3 sc in corner (mark center sc), work 91 (96, 101) sc along lower edge of left front and back, join with sl st to ch 1.
Rnd 2 Ch 3, [skip 4 sc, work shell st in next sc as foll: (2 dc, ch 1, 2 dc) all in one st] 6 (7, 8) times, skip next sc, shell

st in next corner sc, skip next sc, [shell st in next st, skip 4 sc] 6 (7, 8) times, shell st in corner sc, [skip 4 sc, shell st in next sc] 8 (9, 10) times, skip 4 sc, shell st in corner sc, [skip 4 sc, shell st in next sc] 7 times, skip 1 sc, shell st in corner sc, skip 1 sc, [shell st in next sc, skip 4 sc] 18 (19, 20) times, shell st in last sc, join with sl st to top of ch 3. Fasten off.

Shell st border for sleeves

With RS facing and crochet hook, join yarn at lower edge of sleeve.

Rnd 1 Ch 1, work 30 (30, 40) sc evenly along lower edge of sleeve, join with sl st to ch 1.

Rnd 2 Ch 3, *skip 4 sc, work shell st in next sc; rep from * around, end sl st in top of ch 3. ∎

Cardigan Chart

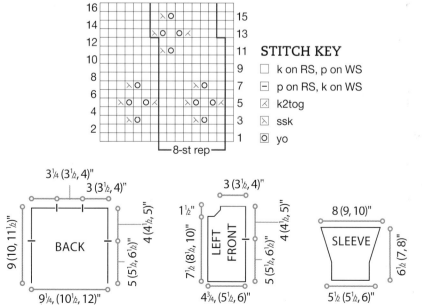

STITCH KEY

☐ k on RS, p on WS

⊟ p on RS, k on WS

⊠ k2tog

⊠ ssk

⊙ yo

GIRL'S LACE
layette

Blanket

MEASUREMENTS
Approximately 30"/76cm square

GAUGE
24 sts and 35 rows to 4"/10cm over St st using size 5 (3.75mm) needles.
Take time to check your gauge.

NOTES
1 Foll the Blanket chart or written instructions below for eyelet pat.
2 K first and last st of every row for selvage st.

EYELET PATTERN
(multiple of 8 sts)
Row 1 (RS) Knit.
Row 2 and all WS rows K1, p to last st, k1.
Row 3 K5, *k2, yo, ssk, k4; rep from * to last 7 sts, k7.
Row 5 K5, *k2tog, yo, k1, yo, ssk, k3; rep from * to last 6 sts, k6.
Row 7 Rep row 3.
Row 9 Knit.
Row 11 K5, *k6, yo, ssk; rep from * to last 11 sts, k11.
Row 13 K6, *k3, k2tog, yo, k1, yo, ssk; rep from * to last 10 sts, k10.
Row 15 Rep row 11.
Row 16 Rep row 2.
Rep rows 1–16 for eyelet pat.

BLANKET
Cast on 168 sts. Work in St st for 8 rows. Work rows 1–16 of eyelet pat once, then work rows 1–8 once more.
Next row (RS) Cont eyelet pat over first 26 sts as established, place marker (pm), work in St st to last 26 sts, pm, cont eyelet pat over last 26 sts.
Cont in pats as established until 16 rows of eyelet pat have been worked

MATERIALS
Yarn (2)
• 12¼oz/350g, 960yd/880m of any sport weight wool yarn in coral

Needles
• One pair size 5 (3.75mm) needles *or size to obtain gauge*

Notions
• Size F/5 (3.75mm) crochet hook
• Stitch markers

I stopped @ 11 rows

13 times at the side edges. Work all sts in eyelet pat, working rows 1–16 once, then rows 1–8 once more. Work all sts in St st for 8 rows. Bind off.

FINISHING
Shell st border
With RS facing and crochet hook, join yarn in first bound-off st.
Rnd 1 Work along bound-off edge as foll: work 3 sc in same st as joining (mark the center st as corner st), work sc2tog over next 2 sts as foll: [insert hook into next st yo and pull up a lp] twice, yo and pull through all 3 lps on hook), [sc in next st, sc2tog] 3 times, [sc in next st, sc2tog, sc in next st] 36 times, [sc2tog, sc in next st] 3 times, sc2tog, 3 sc in last st (mark the center st as corner st), work along side edge as foll: [sc in next row, skip 1 row] 124 times; work along cast-on edge as foll: work 3 sc in first cast-on st (mark the center st as corner st), cont across cast-on sts as for bound-off edge and along 2nd side edge as for other side edge. Join with sl st to first sc.
Rnd 2 Work shell st in first sc as foll: (2 dc, ch 1, 2 dc) all in one st, skip corner st, shell st in next st, *[skip 4 sc, shell st in next st] 24 times, skip 4 sc, shell st in next st, skip next corner st, shell st in next st; rep from * around. Fasten off. ■

Blanket Chart

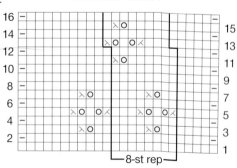

└─8-st rep

STITCH KEY

☐ k on RS, p on WS	⊠ ssk
⊟ p on RS, k on WS	⊙ yo
⊠ k2tog	

Baby hat

SIZES
Sized for Newborn–3 months, 6–9 months, 12–18 months. Shown in 6–9 months.

MEASUREMENTS
Head circumference 13½ (16, 17½)"/34 (40.5, 44.5)cm

GAUGE
24 sts and 35 rows to 4"/10cm over St st using size 5 (3.75mm) needles.
Take time to check your gauge.

HAT
Cast on 80 (96, 104) sts. Divide sts evenly over 4 needles—20 (24, 26) sts on each needle. Join and place marker (pm) for beg of rnd. Work in St st for 8 rnds.
Rnd 1 Knit.
Rnd 2 and all even-numbered rnds, except rnd 12 Knit.
Rnd 3 *K2, yo, ssk, k4; rep from * around.
Rnd 5 *K2tog, yo, k1, yo, ssk, k3; rep from * around.
Rnd 7 Rep rnd 3.
Rnd 9 Knit.
Rnd 11 *K6, yo, ssk; rep from * around.
Rnd 12 *K to last st, sl st to RH needle, remove marker; sl st back to LH needle, ssk, pm for new beg of rnd.
Rnd 13 *K3, k2tog, yo, k1, yo, ssk; rep from * around, end last rep with yo, k1.
Rnd 15 Rep rnd 11.
Rnd 16 Knit.
Rep rnds 1 and 8 once.

MATERIALS
Yarn
- 1¾oz/50g, 140yd/130m of any sport weight wool yarn in coral

Needles
- One set (5) size 5 (3.75mm) double-pointed needles (dpns)
  or size to obtain gauge

Notions
- Stitch marker

Beg top shaping
For size 12–18 months only N=3 mb ?
Next rnd [K11, k2tog] 8 times—96 sts. K 1 rnd.
For sizes 6–9 and 12–18 months only
Next rnd [K10, k2tog] 8 times—88 sts. K 1 rnd.
Next rnd [K9, k2tog] 8 times—80 sts. K 1 rnd.
For all sizes
Next rnd [K8, k2tog] 8 times—72 sts. K 1 rnd.
Next rnd [K7, k2tog] 8 times—64 sts. K 1 rnd.
Cont in this way to dec 8 sts every other rnd, until 8 sts rem.

Top tie
Cont in St st over these 8 sts for approx 2½"/6.5cm. Cut yarn, draw through rem sts and secure. Knot the tie. ■

BABY dress

SIZES
Sized for 3, 6, 12 months. Shown in size 6 months.

MEASUREMENTS
Chest 18 (20, 21½)"/45.5 (50.5, 54.5)cm
Length 12½ (13½, 15)"/31.5 (34.5, 38)cm

GAUGE
26 sts and 36 rows to 4"/10cm over St st using larger needles.
Take time to check your gauge.

K2, P2 RIB
(multiple of 4 sts plus 2)
Row 1 (RS) *K2, p2; rep from *, end k2.
Row 2 K the knit sts and p the purl sts.
Rep row 2 for k2, p2 rib.

BACK
With larger needles, cast on 74 (82, 86) sts. Work in k2, p2 rib for ½"/1.5cm. Work in St st, dec 1 st each side every 8th row 4 (2, 0) times, every 10th row 4 (6, 8) times—58 (66, 70) sts. Work even until piece measures 8½ (9¼, 10)"/21.5 (23.5, 25.5)cm from beg.
Place a marker each side of the center 6 sts.

MATERIALS
Yarn 1
• 3½oz/100g, 450yd/420m (3½oz/100g, 450yd/420m; 5¼oz/150g, 680yd/620m) of any fingering weight acrylic yarn in light orange

Needles
• One pair each sizes 3 and 4 (3.25 and 3.5mm) needles, *or size to obtain gauge*

Notions
• Three sets of small plastic snaps
• Stitch holders
• Stitch markers

Shape sleeves and placket
Inc 1 st each side on next row, then every other row 2 (2, 3) times more, cast on 7 (7, 9) sts at beg of next 2 rows, AT THE SAME TIME, when piece measures 8¾ (9¾, 11½)"/22 (25, 29)cm from beg, bind off the center 6 marked sts, and working both sides at once, complete sleeve incs, then work even on 36 (40, 45) sts each side until placket measures 3"/7.5cm.

Shape neck
Bind off from each neck edge 5 (5, 6) sts once, 3 sts once, 2 (3, 3) sts once. Bind off rem 26 (29, 33) sts each side.

FRONT
Work same as back until piece measures 8¼ (9, 9¾)"/21 (23, 24.5)cm from beg, end with a WS row.

Center rib placket
Next row (RS) K22 (26,28), [p2, k2] 3 times, p2, k22 (26, 28). Cont in pat as established until piece measures 8½ (9¼, 10)"/21.5 (23.5, 25.5)cm from beg.

Shape sleeves
Inc 1 st each side on next row, then every other row 2 (2, 3) times more, then cast on 7 (7, 9) sts at beg of next 2 rows—78 (86, 96) sts.
Work even until rib placket measures 3 (3¼, 4)"/7.5 (8.5, 10)cm, end with a WS row.

Shape neck
Next row (RS) K32 (36, 41), place next 14 rib sts on a holder, join 2nd ball of yarn and k to end. Working both sides at once, bind off from each neck edge 2 (3, 4) sts once, 2 sts twice. Work even until front measures same as back. Bind off rem 26 (29, 33) sts each side.

POCKETS
(make 2)
With smaller needles, cast on 22 sts. Work in k2, p2 rib for 2½"/6.5cm. With larger needle, bind off loosely in rib.

FINISHING
Block pieces to measurements. Sew pockets to front, using photo for placement. Sew shoulder seams.

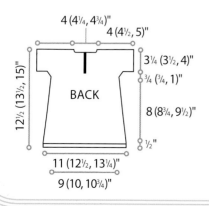

4 (4¼, 4¾)"
4 (4½, 5)"
3¼ (3½, 4)"
¾ (¾, 1)"
12½ (13½, 15)"
BACK
8 (8¾, 9½)"
½"
11 (12½, 13¼)"
9 (10, 10¾)"

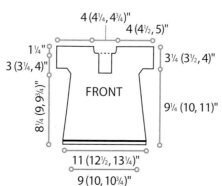

4 (4¼, 4¾)"
4 (4½, 5)"
1¼"
3 (3¼, 4)"
3¼ (3½, 4)"
8¼ (9, 9¾)"
FRONT
9¼ (10, 11)"
11 (12½, 13¼)"
9 (10, 10¾)"

BABY
dress

Back placket bands.

With RS facing and smaller needles, pick up and k 26 sts along right back placket edge. Work in k2, p2 rib for 1"/2.5cm. With larger needle, bind off loosely in rib. Work in same way along left back placket edge. Sew sides of band, left over right, along center 6 bound-off sts.

Neckband

With RS facing and smaller needles, beg at top of left back placket band, pick up and k 34 (36, 38) sts along left back and front neck to sts on holder, rib 14 sts from holder, pick up and k 34 (36, 38) sts along right front and back neck, including side of right back placket band—82 (86, 90) sts. Beg and end with k2 (p2, k2) on next WS row, (to keep center 14 sts in rib as established), work in k2, p2 rib for 1"/2.5cm. With larger needle, bind off loosely in rib.
Sew snaps to placket bands, the first set in the center of the neckband and the other 2 sets spaced evenly apart.

Sleeve bands

With RS facing and smaller needles, pick up and k 46 (50, 58) sts evenly along lower edge of each sleeve. Work in k2, p2 rib for ½"/1.5cm. With larger needle, bind off loosely in rib.
Sew side and under sleeve seams. ■

BABY sunsuit

SIZES
Sized for 3, 6, 12 months. Shown in size 6 months.

MEASUREMENTS
Chest 19 (20, 22)"/48 (50.5, 56)cm
Length 13 (14½, 16)"/33 (36.5, 41)cm

GAUGES
• 26 sts and 36 rows to 4"/10cm over St st using larger needles.
• 30 sts and 36 rows to 4"/10cm over k2, p2 rib, slightly stretched, using larger needles.
Take time to check your gauges.

K2, P2 RIB
(multiple of 4 sts plus 2)
Row 1 (RS) *K2, p2; rep from *, end k2.
Row 2 K the knit sts and p the purl sts.
Rep row 2 for k2, p2 rib.

LEFT BACK LEG
With smaller needles, cast on 28 (30, 34) sts. Work in k2, p2 rib for ½"/1.5cm, dec 0 (0, 1) st on last row—28 (30, 33) sts. Change to larger needles, work in St st as foll: Work 4 rows even. Inc 1 st at beg of next RS row, then rep inc every other row 4 (5, 5) times more times—33 (36, 39) sts.
Work even, if necessary, until piece measures 2 (2½, 2½)"/5 (6.5, 6.5)cm from beg, end with a WS row. Place sts on a holder.

RIGHT BACK LEG
Work to correspond to left back leg, reversing shaping by working incs at end of RS rows. Do not place sts on holder.

MATERIALS

Yarn ①
• 3½oz/100g, 450yd/420m (3½oz/100g, 450yd/420m; 3½oz/100g, 450yd/420m) of any fingering weight acrylic yarn in light orange

Needles
• One pair each sizes 3 and 4 (3.25 and 3.5mm) needles, *or size to obtain gauge*

Notions
• Nine ½"/13mm buttons
• Stitch holders
• Stitch markers

Join legs
Next row (RS) K 33 (36, 39) sts of right back leg, cast on 3 sts, k 33 (36, 39) sts of left back leg—69 (75, 81) sts. P 1 row.
Next (dec) row (RS) K33 (36, 39), SK2P, k33 (36, 39)—67 (73, 79) sts. P 1 row. Rep last 2 rows, working 1 less st before and after center dec, 3 (4, 4) times more—61 (65, 71) sts.
Work even until piece measures 8½ (9½, 10½)"/21.5 (24, 26.5)cm from beg, inc (inc, dec) 1 st at end of last row—62 (66, 70) sts. Change to smaller needles and work in k2, p2 rib for 1"/2.5cm.

25

Shape armhole

Bind off 3 sts at beg of next 4 rows, 2 sts at beg of next 2 rows. Dec I st each side every other row 3 times—40 (44, 48) sts.

Work even until armhole measures 3 (3½, 4)"/7.5 (9, 10)cm.

Shape neck

Next row (RS) Rib 13 (13, 15), join 2nd ball of yarn and bind off center 14 (18, 18) sts, rib to end. Working both sides at once, bind off 2 sts from each neck edge twice. Work even on rem 9 (9, 11) sts each side until armhole measures 4½ (5, 5½)"/11.5 (12.5, 14)cm. Bind off sts each side in rib.

FRONT

Work same as back until armhole measures 1½ (2, 2½)"/4 (5, 6.5)cm.

Shape neck

Next row (RS) Rib 15 (15, 17) sts, join 2nd ball of yarn and bind off center 10 (14, 14) sts, rib to end. Working both sides at once, bind off 2 sts from each neck edge twice, dec I st every other row twice. Work even on rem 9 (9, 11) sts each side until armhole measures 3¼ (3¾, 4¼)"/8.5 (9.5, 11)cm.

On next row, work 2 buttonholes in the center of each shoulder piece as foll:

Next (buttonhole) row (RS) Rib I st, k2tog, yo, rib 2, k2tog, yo, rib to end. Work even until armhole measures 3½ (4, 4½)"/9 (10, 11.5)cm. Bind off sts each side in rib.

POCKETS

(make 2)

With smaller needles, cast on 22 sts. Work in k2, p2 rib for 2½"/6.5cm. With larger needle, bind off loosely in rib.

FINISHING

Block pieces to measurements. Sew pockets to front, using photo for placement. Sew side seams.

Button band

With RS facing and smaller needles, pick up and k 54 (62, 62) sts along back edge of crotch. Work in k2, p2 rib for 1"/2.5cm. With larger needle, bind off loosely in rib. Place markers evenly spaced on band for 5 buttons.

Buttonhole band

Work same as button band, working buttonholes opposite markers on the next RS row by working (k2tog, yo) for each buttonhole.

Neckband

With RS facing and smaller needles, pick up and k 38 (42, 44) sts along back neck edge including along the side edges of button bands. Work 4 rows in k2, p2 rib. Bind off loosely in rib.

With RS facing and smaller needles, pick up and k 46 (50, 50) sts along front neck edge, including along the side edges of buttonhole bands. Work 4 rows in k2, p2 rib. Bind off loosely in rib.

Armhole bands

With RS facing and smaller needles, pick up and k 62 (70, 78) sts around each armhole edge. Work in k2, p2 rib for 1"/2.5cm. With larger needle, bind off loosely in rib.

Sew buttons to back shoulders opposite buttonholes on front. ▪

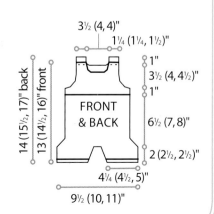

3½ (4, 4)"

1¼ (1¼, 1½)"

14 (15½, 17)" back

13 (14½, 16)" front

1"

3½ (4, 4½)"

1"

FRONT & BACK

6½ (7, 8)"

2 (2½, 2½)"

4¼ (4½, 5)"

9½ (10, 11)"

BABY cardigan

SIZES
Sized for 3, 6, 12 months. Shown in 6 months.

MEASUREMENTS
Chest (buttoned) 19½ (21½, 23)"/49.5 (54.5, 58.5)cm
Length 9½ (10½, 12)"/24 (26.5, 30.5)cm
Upper arm 8 (8½, 9½)"/20.5 (21.5, 24)cm

GAUGE
26 sts and 36 rows to 4"/10cm over St st using size larger needles.
Take time to check your gauge.

K2, P2 RIB
(multiple of 4 sts plus 2)
Row 1 (RS) *K2, p2; rep from *, end k2.
Row 2 K the knit sts and p the purl sts. Rep row 2 for k2, p2 rib.

K2, P2 RIB
(multiple of 4 sts)
Row 1 (RS) K3, *p2, k2; rep from *, end k3.
Row 2 K the knit sts and p the purl sts. Rep row 2 for k2, p2 rib.

BACK
With smaller needles, cast on 64 (70, 76) sts. Work in k2, p2 rib for ½"/1.5cm. Change to larger needles and work in St st until piece measures 5½ (6, 7)"/14 (15, 17.5)cm from beg.

Shape armhole
Bind off 3 (4, 4) sts at beg of next 2 rows. Dec 1 st each side every other row 3 times—52 (56, 62) sts. Work even until armhole measures 4 (4½, 5)"/10 (11.5, 12.5)cm. Bind off all sts.

MATERIALS
Yarn ❶
• 3½oz/100g, 450yd/420m (3½oz/100g, 450yd/420m; 3½oz/100g, 450yd/420m) of any fingering weight acrylic yarn in light orange

Needles
• One pair each sizes 3 and 4 (3.25 and 3.5mm) needles, *or size to obtain gauge*

Notions
• 3 (3, 4) ½"/13mm buttons
• One set of small plastic snaps
• Stitch markers

LEFT FRONT
With smaller needles cast on 44 (48, 52) sts. Work in k2, p2 rib for ½"/1.5cm. Change to larger needles and work in St st until piece measures 5½ (6, 7)"/14 (15, 17.5)cm from beg, end with a WS row.

Shape armhole
Bind off from armhole edge (beg of RS rows) 3 (4, 4) sts once, dec 1 st every other row 3 times—38 (41, 45) sts. Work even until armhole measures 2 (2½, 3)"/5 (6.5, 7.5)cm, end with a RS row.

Shape neck
Next row (WS) Bind off 14 (16, 17) sts (neck edge), work to end. Cont to bind off from neck edge 3 sts 3 times, dec 1 st every other row twice. Work even on rem 13 (14, 17) sts until armhole measures same as back. Bind off sts for shoulder.

RIGHT FRONT
Work to correspond to left front, reversing all shaping by working armhole bind offs at beg of WS rows and neck bind offs at beg of RS rows.

SLEEVES
With smaller needles, cast on 36 (40, 42) sts. Work in k2, p2 rib for ½"/1cm. Change to larger needles and work in St st, inc 1 st each side every 4th row 8 (3, 3) times, every 0 (6th 6th) row 0 (5, 7) times—52 (56, 62) sts. Work even until piece measures 5 (6, 7½)"/12.5 (15.5, 19)cm from beg.

Shape cap
Bind off 3 (4, 4) sts at beg of next 2 rows. Dec 1 st each side every other row 5 (7, 8) times. Bind off 5 (5, 4) sts at beg of next 4 rows, 5 (4, 4) sts at beg of next 2 (2, 4) rows. Bind off rem 6 sts.

POCKET
With smaller needles, cast on 22 sts. Work in k2, p2 rib for 2½"/6.5cm. With larger needle, bind off loosely in rib.

FINISHING
Block pieces to measurements. Sew pocket to right front, using photo for placement. Sew shoulder seams.

Neckband
With RS facing and smaller needles, beg at right front neck, pick up and k 32 (34, 36) sts along right front neck, 26 (28, 30) sts along back neck and 32 (34, 36) sts along left front neck—90 (96, 102) sts. Work in k2, p2 rib for ½"/1.5cm. With larger needle, bind off loosely in rib.

Left front band
With RS facing and smaller needles, pick up and k 54 (60, 70) sts along left front edge, inlcuding side of neckband. Work in k2, p2 rib for ½"/1.5cm.

Jack Deutsch

Right front buttonhole band
Work as for left front band, working
buttonholes on next RS row as foll:
Buttonhole row (RS) Rib 14 (20, 12),
[k2tog, yo, rib 16] 2 (2, 3) times, k2tog,
yo, rib 2. Complete as for left front band.
Sew buttons to left front, opposite
buttonholes and 4¼ (4¾, 5)"/10.5 (12,
12.5)cm in from front edge. Sew bottom
half of snap to top of left front neck and
the top half of snap to the correspond-
ing place on WS of right front neckband
when cardigan is buttoned.
Set in sleeves. Sew side and sleeve
seams. ▪

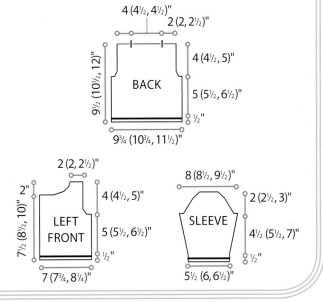

BACK
4 (4½, 4½)"
2 (2, 2½)"
4 (4½, 5)"
5 (5½, 6½)"
½"
9½ (10½, 12)"
9¾ (10¾, 11½)"

LEFT FRONT
2 (2, 2½)"
2"
7½ (8½, 10)"
4 (4½, 5)"
5 (5½, 6½)"
½"
7 (7¾, 8¼)"

SLEEVE
8 (8½, 9½)"
2 (2½, 3)"
4½ (5½, 7)"
½"
5½ (6, 6½)"

CABLED hat

SIZES
Sized for Baby, Toddler, and Child.
Shown in size Toddler.

MEASUREMENTS
Head circumference 14½ (16, 18½)"/37 (40.5, 47)cm
Length 6 (6½, 6½)"/15 (16.5, 16.5)cm

GAUGES
• 26 sts and 32 rows to 4"/10cm over cable pat using larger needles.
• 24 sts and 32 rows to 4"/10cm over k2, p2 rib using larger needles.
Take time to check your gauges.

STITCH GLOSSARY
2-st RC Sl 1 to cn and hold to *back*, k1, k1 from cn.
2-st LC Sl 1 to cn and hold to *front*, k1, k1 from cn.

CABLE PATTERN
(multiple of 8 sts)
Rnds 1–3 *P1, k4, p1, k2; rep from * around.
Rnd 4 *P1, 2-st LC, 2-st RC, p1, 2-st LC; rep from * around.
Rep rnds 1–4 for cable pat.

K2, P2 RIB
(multiple of 4 sts)
Rnd 1 *K2, p2; rep from * around.
Rep rnd 1 for k2, p2 rib.

HAT
With circular needle, cast on 88 (96, 112) sts. Place marker (pm) for beg of rnd and join, taking care not to twist sts. Work in k2, p2 rib until piece measures 1¼"/3cm from beg.

MATERIALS
Yarn 〔4〕
• 1¾oz/50g, 160yd/150m (3½oz/100g, 310yd/280m; 3½oz/100g, 310yd/280m) of any worsted weight cotton and acrylic blend yarn in light yellow

Needles
• One size 6 (4mm) circular needle, 12"/30cm long *or size to obtain gauge*
• One set (5) size 6 (4mm) double-pointed needles (dpns)
• Two size 5 (3.75mm) double-pointed needles (dpns)

Notions
• Stitch marker

Beg cable pat
Beg with rnd 1, work cable pat 11 (12, 14) times around until piece measures 6¼ (6¾, 6¾)"/16 (17, 17)cm from beg, end with a rnd 4.

Shape crown
Note Change to dpns when sts no longer fit comfortably on circular needle.
Next (dec) rnd *K2tog tbl, k3, p1, k2; rep from * around—77 (84, 98) sts.
Next rnd *K4, p1, k2; rep from * around.
Next (dec) rnd *K4, k2tog tbl, k1; rep from * around—66 (72, 84) sts.
Next rnd *2-st LC, 2-st RC, 2-st LC; rep from * around.
Next (dec) rnd *K4, k2tog; rep from * around.
Next rnd Knit.
Next (dec) rnd *K3, k2tog; rep from * around.
Next rnd Knit.
Next (dec) rnd *K2, k2tog; rep from * around.

Next (dec) rnd *K1, k2tog; rep from * around.
Next (dec) rnd *K2tog; rep from * around—11 (12, 14) sts.
Break yarn, leaving long tail. Thread tail through rem sts twice. Fasten off.

Earflaps
Fold ribbed brim to RS and pm along fold at beg of rnd for center back. Pm 2¾ (3, 3½)"/7 (7.5, 9)cm from back marker on either side of hat. With size 5 (3.75mm) dpn and RS facing, pick up and k 15 (17, 19) sts along fold beg at right side marker, working away from back marker and picking up 1 st in each st along fold. Work in garter st (k every row) until earflap measures 1½"/4cm.
Next (dec) row K2, SKP, k to last 4 sts, k2tog, k2.
Next row Knit.
Rep last 2 rows 4 (5, 6) times more— 5 sts.
Next (dec) row K1, SK2P, k1—3 sts.
Work I-cord over rem 3 sts as foll: *Knit one row. Without turning work, slide the sts back to the opposite end of needle to work next from RS. Pull yarn tightly from the end of the row. Rep from * until I-cord measures approx 10"/25.5cm. Bind off.
With size 5 (3.75mm) dpns and WS facing, pick up and k 15 (17, 19) sts along fold beg at left side marker, working away from back marker and picking up 1 st in each st along fold. Complete as for right earflap. ■

LAYETTE quintet

SIZES
Sized for 3, 6, 9 months. Shown in size 9 months.

MEASUREMENTS
Slippers
Length 3½ (4, 4¾)"/9 (10, 12)cm

Hat
Circumference 14 (15¾, 17¼)"/35.5 (40, 44)cm
Length 5½ (6¾, 6¾)"/14 (17, 17)cm

Pants
Waist 22 (24, 24)"/56 (61, 61)cm
Length 14 (14¼, 15)"/35.5 (37, 38)cm

Cardigan
Chest (closed) 22 (23, 24)"/56 (58.5, 61)cm
Length 10 (11, 12½)"/25.5 (28, 31.5)cm
Upper arm 9 (10, 11)"/23 (25.5, 28)cm

GAUGES
• 24 sts and 32 rows/rnds to 4"/10cm over St st.
• 24 sts and 38 rows/rnds to 4"/10cm over seed st.
Take time to check your gauges.

SEED STITCH
(over an even number of sts)
Row 1 *K1, p1; rep from * to end.
Row 2 K the purl sts and p the knit sts.
Rep row 2 for seed st.

I-CORD
Cast on 1 st. (K1, p1, k1, p1) in first st. *K one row. Without turning work, slip the sts back to beg of the row. Pull yarn tightly from the end of the row. Rep from * to given measurement. K4tog through back loops.

MATERIALS
Yarn 3
Any DK weight cotton yarn
• 14oz/400g, 990yd/910m (14oz/400g, 990yd/910m; 15¾oz/450g, 1110yd/1020m) in purple (A)
• 3½oz/100g, 250yd/230m in light yellow (B)

Needles
• One each size 5 (3.75mm) circular needle, 16"/40cm and 29"/74cm lengths *or size to obtain gauge*
• One set (5) size 5 (3.75mm) double-pointed needles (dpns)

Notions
• Three ½"/13mm snaps
• Tapestry needle
• Stitch markers and holder

ATTACHED I-CORD TRIM
With dpns, cast on 3 sts, then *pick up one st on edge of piece to make 4 sts. Slide sts to opposite end of dpn and k2, then k2tog through the back loops. Rep from *.

Slippers
SOLE
With A, cast on 15 (19, 21) sts. Working in seed st, inc 1 st at beg of next 6 (6, 8) rows—21 (25, 29) sts. Work 4 rows even. Dec 1 st at beg of next 6 (6, 8) rows—15 (19, 21) sts.

UPPER
Next row (RS) Cast on 6 (6, 8) sts at beg of row for heel, work to end of row—21 (25, 29) sts.
Next (inc) row (WS) Inc 1 st for toe, work to end of row. Work inc row every other row 4 times more—26 (30, 34) sts.

Next row (RS) Bind off 11 (15, 17) sts, work to end of row—15 (15, 17) sts. Work even for 9 rows.
Next row (RS) Cast on 11 (15, 17) sts, work to end of row—26 (30, 34) sts.
Next (dec) row (WS) Dec 1 st, work to end of row. Rep dec row every other row 4 times more—21 (25, 29) sts. Bind off.

FINISHING
Sew tog back seam of heel. Sew sole to lower edge of upper. With RS facing, work I-cord trim in B around foot opening of slipper. Make second slipper as for first.

Hat
With dpns and A, cast on 84 (94, 104) sts. Place marker (pm) and join for beg of rnd, taking care not to twist sts. Work in seed st for 1 (1¼, 1¼)"/2.5 (3, 3cm). Change to St st and inc 6 sts evenly around—90 (100, 110) sts. Work until piece measures 5 (6¼, 6¼)"/12.5 (16, 16)cm from beg.

Shape crown
Next (dec) rnd Dec 10 (4, 14) sts evenly spaced around—80 (96, 96) sts.
Next (dec) rnd *K2, k2tog; rep from * around—60 (72, 72) sts. Work 1 rnd even.
Next (dec) rnd *K1, k2tog; rep from * around—40 (48, 48) sts. Work 1 rnd even.
Next 2 (dec) rnds *K2tog; rep from * around—10 (12, 12) sts.
Cut yarn leaving 12"/30.5cm tail. Thread through rem sts and cinch tightly to close.

FINISHING
With B and RS facing, work attached I-cord trim around lower edge of hat. Make a 2½"/6.5cm length I-cord, tie into a knot and attach to top of hat.

LAYETTE quintet

Pants

LEG

With dpns and A, cast on 48 (52, 54) sts. Pm and join for beg of rnd, taking care not to twist sts. Work in seed st for ¾"/2cm. Change to St st (k every row) and inc 12 stitches evenly around—60 (64, 66) sts. Work even until piece measures 6¾ (7, 7¼)"/17 (18, 18.5)cm from beg. Place on holder. Work second leg as for first.

Join legs

With 16"/40cm circular needle, work 30 (32, 33) sts of first leg, cast on 8 sts, work 60 (64, 66) sts of second leg, cast on 8 sts, work rem 30 (32, 33) sts of first leg—136 (144, 148) sts.
Pm and join for beg of rnd. Work in St st until piece measures 6½ (6½, 7)"/6.5 (16.5, 18)cm above joining rnd.
Next rnd Dec 4 (0, 4) sts evenly around—132 (144, 144) sts.
Change to seed st and work 3 rnds.
Next rnd *Work 4 sts, k or p2tog, yo; rep from * around to form eyelet holes for tie. Work 3 more rnds in seed st. Bind off. chro
With B, knit I-cord 28 (28½, 29½)"/71 (72.5, 75)cm long. Thread through the eyelet holes, beg and ending at the middle of the front. Tie knots in ends of cord, and pull to gather top.

FINISHING

With B and RS facing, work attached I-cord trim around lower edges of legs.

Sweater

LEFT FRONT

With A, cast on 38 (40, 42) sts. Work in seed st until piece measures 5½ (6, 7)"/14 (15, 18)cm, end with a WS row.

Shape sleeve

Next row (RS) Cast on 6 sts, work to end of row—42 (46, 48) sts.
Cast on 6 sts at beg of next 5 (5, 6) RS rows, then 3 sts 0 (1, 0) times, AT THE SAME TIME, when piece measures 6 (6½, 7½)"/15 (16.5, 19)cm from beg, shape neck at beg of WS rows as foll:

Neck shaping

Bind off 4 sts once, 2 sts once. Dec 1 st at beg of WS rows 11 (11, 12) times—57 (62, 66) sts.

When piece measures 10 (11,12½)"/25.5 (28, 31.5)cm from beg, place sts on holder.

RIGHT FRONT

Work right front in the same manner and reverse shaping by working sleeve incs at beg of WS rows and neck shaping at beg of RS rows.

Join for the back

With RS facing, work across the left sleeve and front, cast on 24 sts for back neck, then work across the right sleeve and front—138 (148, 156) sts. Work until piece measures 4½ (5, 5½)"/11.5 (12.5, 14)cm from joining row.

Shape sleeve
Bind off 6 sts at beg of next 12 (12, 14) rows, then 3 sts at beg of next 0 (1, 0) row—66 (70, 72) sts. Work even until piece measures 10 (11, 12½)"/25.5 (28, 31.5)cm from neck joining row and bind off.

FINISHING
Sew seam from cuff to bottom of sweater, leaving 1¼"/3cm open at bottom of sweater. With B and RS facing, beg at lower right front edge, work I-cord trim around entire edge,

then at each sleeve edge. Make three 9"/23cm I-cord ties and knot each end. Tie in double knot and sew to left front edge as foll: Place top knot 1½"/4cm from neck shaping, lowest knot 1"/2.5cm from lower edge and one centered between. Sew snaps even with knots on underside of Left Front and front side of Right Front. ■

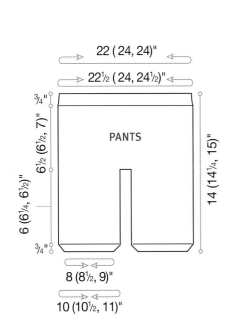

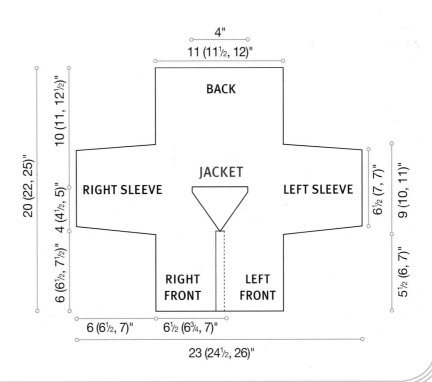

Blanket

SIZES
One size.

MEASUREMENTS
Approximately 29 x 20"/73.5 x 51cm

GAUGE
22 sts and 30 rows to 4"/10cm over St st using size 3 (3.25) needles.
Take time to check your gauge.

STITCH GLOSSARY
3-st RPC Sl next st to cn and hold to *back*, k2, p1 from cn.
3-st LPC Sl 2 sts to cn and hold to *front*, p1, k2 from cn.
4-st RC Sl 2 sts to cn and hold to *back*, k2, k2 from cn.
4-st LC Sl 2 sts to cn and hold to *front*, k2, k2 from cn.
4-st RPC Sl 2 st to cn and hold to *back*, k2, p2 from cn.
4-st LPC Sl 2 sts to cn and hold to *front*, p2, k2 from cn.
5-st LC Sl 3 sts to cn and hold to *front*, k2, k3 from cn.
5-st LPC Sl 2 sts to cn and hold to *front*, k2, p1, k2 from cn.

DOUBLE SEED STITCH
(over an odd number of sts)
Row 1 (RS) *K1, p1; rep from * , end k1.
Row 2 K the knit sts and p the purl sts.
Row 3 *P1, k1; rep from * , end p1.
Row 4 P the purl sts and k the knit sts.
Rep rows 1–4 for double seed stitch.

BLANKET
Cast on 161 sts. Work 6 rows in double seed st.
Next row (RS) Work 6 sts in double seed st as established, k to last 6 sts, work 6 sts in double seed st.

MATERIALS

Yarn (3)
• 8¾oz/250g, 690yd/640m of any DK weight wool blend yarn in green

Needles
• One pair size 3 (3.25mm) needles
or size to obtain gauge

Notions
• Cable needle (cn) and stitch markers

Next row (WS) Work 6 sts in double seed st, p to last 6 sts, work 6 sts in double seed st.
Next row (RS) Work 6 sts in double seed st, k68, 4-st RPC for traveling cable, 5-st LC, 4-st LPC for traveling cable, k to the last 6 sts, work double seed st to end.
Next row and all WS rows K the knit sts and p the purl sts.
Next row (RS) Work 6 sts in double seed st, k66, 4-st RPC, p2, k5, p2, 4-st LPC, k to last 6 sts, work in double seed st to end. Work WS row.
Next row (RS) Work 6 sts in double seed st, k64, 4-st RPC, p4, 5-st LPC, p4, 4-st LPC, work to end.
Next (set-up) row (WS) Work 72 sts in pat, place marker (pm), k8, p1, k8, pm, work in pat to end.

Beg chart
Next row (RS) Work to 4 sts before marker, 4-st RPC, sl marker, work row 1 of 17-st chart, sl marker, 4-st LPC.
Next row K the knit sts and p the purl sts.
Next row (RS) Work to 6 sts before marker, 4-st RPC, p to marker, sl marker, work chart row 3, sl marker, p2, 4-st LPC work to end.
Cont to work in this manner, foll chart and working 2 fewer k sts before each 4-st RPC, and 2 more p sts before each 4-st LPC until rows 1–26 of chart have been completed twice. Cont in pat as

established and rep rows 1–14 of chart once more. All of the sts between the traveling cables and the center cable panel have been worked into rev st.
Next row (RS) Work 6 sts in double seed st, 4-st LC, p to marker, work chart row 15, p to 4 sts before double seed st edge, 4-st RC, work in pat to end. Cont in this manner, working 2 more k sts before 4-st LC and 2 fewer p sts before 4-st RC until chart pat has been worked through row 26 for 4 times total and rows 1–25 have been worked once more.
Next row (WS) Work 6 sts double seed st, p66, remove marker, k6, p5, k to next marker, remove marker, p to last 6 sts, work in double seed st to end.
Next row (RS) Work 6 sts in double seed st, k64, 4-st LC, p4, k5, p4, 4-st RC, k to last 6 sts, work in pat to end.
Next row K the knit sts and p the purl sts.
Next row (RS) Work 6 sts in double seed st, k66, 4-st LC, p2, k5, p2, 4-st RC, k to last 6 sts, work in pat to end.
Next row K the knit sts and p the purl sts.
Next row (RS) Work 6 sts in double seed st, k68, 4-st LC, 5-st LPC, 4-st RC, k to last 6 sts, work in pat to end.
Next row Work 6 sts in pat, p to last 6 sts, work to end.
Work 6 rows in double seed st.
Bind off in pat. ■

STITCH KEY

☐ k on RS, p on WS

▨ p on RS, k on WS

◣◥ 3-st RPC

◢◣ 3-st LPC

◢◣◥ 5-st LPC

17 sts

BOY'S layette

Cardi

SIZES
Sized for Newborn–3 months, 6–9, 12–18 months. Shown in 6–9 months.

MEASUREMENTS
Chest (buttoned) 19 (20¼, 22½)"/48 (51.5, 57)cm
Length 9½ (10½, 12)"/24 (26.5, 30.5)cm
Upper arm 8 (9, 10)"/ 20.5 (23, 25.5)cm

GAUGE
22 sts and 30 rows to 4"/10cm over St st using size 3 (3.25) needles.
Take time to check your gauge.

STITCH GLOSSARY
3-st RPC Sl next st to cn and hold to *back*, k2, p1 from cn.
3-st LPC Sl 2 sts to cn and hold to *front*, p1, k2 from cn.
5-st LPC Sl 2 sts to cn and hold to *front*, k2, p1, k2 from cn.

DOUBLE SEED STITCH
(over an odd number of sts)
Row 1 (RS) *K1, p1; rep from * , end k1.
Row 2 K the knit sts and p the purl sts.
Row 3 *P1, k1; rep from *, end p1.
Row 4 P the purl sts and k the knit sts.
Rep rows 1–4 for double seed stitch.

DOUBLE SEED STITCH
(over an even number of sts)
Row 1 (RS) *K1, p1; rep from * to end.
Row 2 Rep row 1.
Row 3 *P1, k1; rep from * to end.
Row 4 Rep row 4.
Rep rows 1–4 for double seed stitch.

BACK
Cast on 55 (57, 63) sts. Work 5 rows in double seed st.

MATERIALS
Yarn (3)
• 5¼oz/150g, 420yd/390m
(5¼oz/150g, 420yd/390m; 7oz/200g, 550yd/510m) of any DK weight wool blend yarn in green

Needles
• One pair size 3 (3.25mm) needles
or size to obtain gauge

Notions
• Cable needle (cn) and stitch markers
• Five ½"/12mm buttons

Change to St st (k on RS, p on WS) and work until piece measures 6 (7,8)"/15 (18, 20.5)cm from beg, end with a WS row.

Shape armholes
Bind off 3 sts at beg of next 2 rows, 2 sts at beg of next 2 rows—45 (47. 53) sts. Work even until armhole measures 3 (3, 3½)"/7.5 (7.5, 9)cm from beg.

Shape neck
Next row (RS) K18 (19, 21), join 2nd ball of yarn and bind off next 9 (9, 11) sts, k to end.
Working both sides at once, bind off 2 sts at each neck edge. Bind off rem 16 (17, 19) sts each side.

LEFT FRONT
Cast on 33 (34, 38) sts. Work 4 rows in double seed st.
Next (buttonhole) row (RS) Work in pat to last 4 sts, k2tog, yo, work to end. Rep button hole row every 12th (14th 16th) row 4 times more. AT THE SAME TIME begin cable pattern.

Beg chart
Set-up row (WS) Work 6 sts in double seed st as established for button band, place marker (pm), p3, k5, p5, k5, pm, p to end.
Next row (RS) K to marker, sl marker, work row 1 of chart pat, k3, sl marker, work in pat to end.
Cont to work chart in this manner until ✳ row 16 of chart is complete. Rep rows 1–16 until piece measures same as back to armhole, end with a WS row. *RS on Rt sm*

Shape armhole *WS on Rt side*
Next row (RS) Bind off 3 sts, work in pats to end—30 (31, 35) sts.
Work 1 row in pat.
Next row (RS) Bind off 2 sts, work to end—28 (29, 33) sts.
Work even as established until piece measures 7½ (8½, 10)"/19 (21.5, 25.5) cm from beg, end with a WS row.

Shape neck
Cont in pat, bind off at neck edge as foll: 6 (6, 8) sts once, 4 sts once, 2 sts once—16 (17, 19) sts. Work even until piece measures same as back. Bind off.

RIGHT FRONT
Work same as for left front, reversing shaping and omitting buttonholes.

SLEEVES
Cast on 34 (36, 38) sts. Work 5 rows double seed st.
Next row (WS) Purl to end.
Next (inc) row (RS) Kfb, k to last 2 sts, kfb, k1—36 (38, 40) sts.
Cont in St st, rep inc row every 8th (6th, 6th) row 4 (6, 7) times more—44 (50, 54) sts.
Work even until piece measures 6 (6½, 7½)"/15 (16.5, 19)cm from beg.

Shape armhole

Bind off 3 sts at beg of next 2 rows—38 (44, 48) sts. Bind off 2 sts at beg of next 2 rows—34 (40, 44) sts. Bind off rem sts.

HOOD

Cast on 88 (88, 94) sts. Work 5 rows in double seed st. Work in St st until piece measures 5 (5, 6)"/12.5 (12.5, 15)cm. Bind off 12 sts at beg of next 6 rows. Bind off rem 16 (16, 22) sts. Fold in half and sew bound-off edges tog.

FINISHING

Sew shoulder seams. Set in sleeves. Sew cast-on edge of hood to neck edges of body. Sew side and sleeve seams. Sew on buttons opposite buttonholes. ■

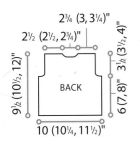

2¾ (3, 3¼)"
2½ (2½, 2¾)"
9½ (10½, 12)"
BACK
3½ (3½, 4)"
6 (7, 8)"
10 (10¼, 11½)"

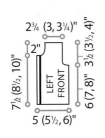

2¾ (3, 3¼)"
2"
7½ (8½, 10)"
LEFT FRONT
3½ (3½, 4)"
6 (7, 8)"
5 (5½, 6)"

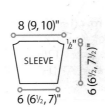

8 (9, 10)"
SLEEVE
½"
6 (6½, 7½)"
6 (6½, 7)"

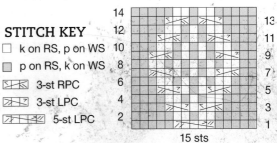

STITCH KEY

□	k on RS, p on WS
▨	p on RS, k on WS
⧄⧅	3-st RPC
⧄	3-st LPC
⧄⧄	5-st LPC

15 sts

BOY'S layette

Pants

SIZES

Sized for Newborn–3 months, 6–9, 12–18 months. Shown in 6–9 months.

MEASUREMENTS

Waist 18 (20, 20½)"/45.5 (51, 52)cm
Hips 23½ (24½, 26½)"/57 (62, 67)cm
Length outer leg to waistband 11½ (13½, 16)"/29 (34, 40.5)cm

GAUGE

22 sts and 30 rows to 4"/10cm over St st using size 3 (3.25mm) needles.
Take time to check your gauge.

DOUBLE SEED STITCH

(over an even number of sts)
Rows 1 and 2 *K1, p1; rep from * to end.
Rows 3 and 4 *P1, k1; rep from * to end.
Rep rows 1–4 for double seed stitch.

BACK

Cast on 30 (32, 34) sts for leg. With 2nd ball of yarn, cast on 30 (32, 34) sts for 2nd leg. Working both legs at once, work 5 rows in double seed stitch.
Next row (RS) K to last 5 sts, work 5 sts in double seed st as established.
With 2nd ball of yarn, work 5 sts in double seed st as established, k to end.
Work even in pat until legs measure 5 (6, 7½)"/12.5 (15, 19)cm from beg, end with a WS row.
Next (joining) row (RS) Work 30 (32, 34) sts of first leg in pat, cont with same ball of yarn, cast on 4 sts and work 30 (32, 34) sts of 2nd leg in pat—64 (68, 72) sts.
Next row (WS) P25 (27, 29), work next 14 sts in double seed st as established, p to end.

MATERIALS

Yarn ③

• 5¼oz/150g, 420yd/390m
(5¼oz/150g, 420yd/390m;
8¾oz/250g, 690yd/640m) of any DK weight wool blend yarn in green

Needles

• One pair size 3 (3.25mm) needles
or size to obtain gauge

Notions

• 7 (7, 9) ½"/12mm buttons
• Stitch markers

Next row (RS) K26 (28, 30) work next 12 sts in double seed st, k to end.
Work 1 row in pat.
Next row (RS) K28 (30, 32) work next 8 sts in double seed st, k to end.
Work 1 row in pat.
Next row (RS) K30 (32, 34), work next 4 sts in double seed st, k to end. Work 1 row in pat.
Next row (RS) Knit.
Cont in St st (k on RS, p on WS) for ½ (1, 1½)"/1.5 (2.5, 4)cm, end with a WS row.

Shape waist

Next (dec) row (RS) K15 (16, 17), k2tog, place marker (pm), k30 (32, 34), pm, ssk, k to end—62 (66, 70) sts.
Purl one row.
Next (dec) row K to 2 sts before marker, k2tog, sl marker, k to next marker, sl marker, ssk, k to end—60 (64, 68) sts.
Rep dec row every other row 5 (5, 6) times more—50 (54, 56) sts.
Work even in St st until piece measures 6 (6½, 7½"/15 (16.5, 19)cm from joining row, end with a RS row.

Waistband

Work 5 rows in double seed st. Bind off in pat.

FRONT

Cast on 30 (32, 34) sts for leg. With 2nd ball of yarn, cast on 30 (32, 34) sts for 2nd leg. Working both legs at once, work 5 rows in double seed stitch.
Next (buttonhole) row (RS) K25 (27, 29) work 1 st in double seed st as established, k2tog, yo, work 2 sts in pat, with 2nd ball of yarn, work 2 sts in double seed st, yo, k2tog, work 1 st in pat, k to end.
Cont to work same as for back, rep buttonhole row every 16th (18th, 16th) row 2 (2, 3) times more. When piece measures 5 (6, 7½)"/12.5 (15, 19)cm from beg, join same as for back. Work as for back until there are 12 sts worked in double seed stitch at center.
Next (buttonhole) row (RS) K28 (30, 32), work 3 sts in double seed st, k2tog, yo, work 3 sts in double seed st, k to end.
Cont as for back until Shape waist.

Shape waist

Next (dec) row (RS) K2, ssk, k to last 4 sts, k2tog, k2—62 (66, 70) sts.
Rep dec row every other row 6 (6, 7) times more—50 (54, 56) sts.
Work even in St st until piece measures 6 (6½, 7½)"/15 (16.5, 19)cm from joining row, end with a WS row.

Waistband

Work 2 rows in double seed st.
Next (buttonhole) row (RS) Work 16 (18, 19) sts in double seed st as established, k2tog, yo, work 14 sts in seed st, yo, k2tog, work in double seed st to end.
Work 2 rows more in double seed st as established. Bind off in pat.

SUSPENDERS

Cast on 6 sts. Work in double seed stitch until strap measures 11 (13, 15)"/28 (33, 38)cm from beg. Bind off in pat.

FINISHING

Sew side seams. Sew straps to WS of back waistband. Sew buttons to legs and straps to correspond to buttonholes. ◼

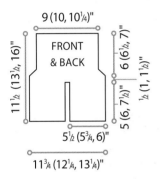

9 (10, 10¼)"

FRONT
& BACK

11½ (13½, 16)"

6 (6½, 7)"

5 (6, 7½)"

½ (1, 1½)"

5½ (5¾, 6)"

11¾ (12¼, 13¼)"

TINY treasures

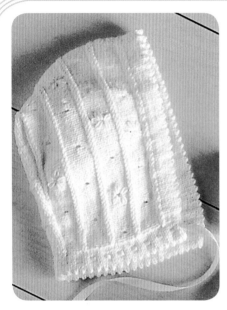

PATTERN STITCH

multiple of 9 plus 6 (12, 9, 6)
Rows 1 and 13 (RS) Purl.
Rows 2 and 14 Knit
Rows 3, 5, 9, 11, 15, 17, 21 and 23 Knit.
Rows 4, 6, 8, 10, 12, 16, 18, 20 and 22 Purl.
Row 7 K2 (0, 3, 2), k2tog, *yo, k7, k2tog; rep from *, end yo, k2 (1, 4, 2).
Row 19 K3 (1, 4, 3) *k4, k2tog, yo, k3; rep from *, end last rep k6 (5, 8, 6).
Row 24 Purl.
Rep rows 1–24 for pat st.

BONNET

With smaller needles cast on 96 (102, 108, 114) sts. Work in St st for ¾"/2cm, end with a WS row. Change to larger needles.
Eyelet turning row (RS) K1, *k2tog, yo; rep from * to last st, k1.
Work in St st for ¾"/2cm. Work in pat st until piece measures 4¾ (5, 5¼, 5½)"/12 (12.5, 13, 13.5)cm above eyelet row.

Top shaping

Bind off 5 (5, 6, 7) sts at beg of next 8 (4, 4, 4) rows, 6 sts at beg of next 4 (8, 8, 8) rows—32 (34, 36, 38) sts. Dec 1 st each side [every 4th row once, every 5th row once] 4 (4, 4, 5) times, every 4th row 0 (1, 1, 0) time—16 (16, 18, 18) sts. Work even until piece measures 9½ (10, 10¼, 10½)"/24 (25, 26, 27)cm above eyelet row. Place sts on a holder.

FINISHING

Block piece. Fold in half and sew open sts tog for back seam. Fold at eyelet row to WS and sew hem in place for picot edge.

Lower edging

With RS facing and larger needles, pick up and k 74 (76, 80, 84) sts evenly along lower edge, including side of picot edge. Work in St st for ¾"/2cm. Work eyelet turning ridge as before. Change to smaller needles, work in St st for ¾"/2cm more. Bind off. Fold edging to WS

at eyelet row and sew in place. Weave ribbon through center of band. Make two ¾"/2cm pompoms and sew to each end of ribbon. Embroider flowers using lazy daisy st (see photo for placement).

MATERIALS

Yarn 1

Any fingering weight cotton yarn,
• 5¼oz/150g, 590yd/540m (5¼oz/150g, 590yd/540m; 7oz/200g, 780yd/720m; 7oz/200g, 780yd/720m) in white

Needles

• One pair size 2 (2.5mm) needles *or size to obtain gauge*

Notions

• Size B/1 (2mm) crochet hook
• 2yd/2m satin ribbon, ¼"/6mm wide

Surplice wrap shirt

SIZES

Sized for Newborn, 6, 12, 18 months. Shown in size Newborn.

MEASUREMENTS

Chest (closed) 22 (23½, 25, 27)"/56 (59.5, 63.5, 68.5)cm
Length 10¼ (11, 11¾, 12¾)"/26 (28, 30, 32)cm
Upper arm 10 (10½, 11½, 12¼)"/25.5 (27, 29, 31)cm

GAUGE

30 sts and 44 rows to 4"/10cm over chart 1 using size 2 (2.5mm) needles. *Take time to check your gauge.*

NOTE

Be sure that there is always a yo to compensate for each dec in every row to keep st count the same. If there is not, then omit the yo or dec and work in St st.

MATERIALS

Yarn 1

Any fingering weight cotton yarn,
• 1¾oz/50g, 200yd/190m (1¾oz/50g, 200yd/190m; 1¾oz/50g, 200yd/190m; 3½oz/100g, 390yd/360m) in white

Needles

• One pair sizes 1 and 2 (2.25 and 2.5mm) needles *or size to obtain gauge*

Notions

• 31½"/80cm satin ribbon, ¼"/6mm wide
• Stitch holder

Bonnet

SIZES

Sized for Newborn, 6, 12, 18 months. Shown in size Newborn.

GAUGE

30 sts and 44 rows to 4"/10cm over pat st using larger needles. *Take time to check your gauge.*

BACK

Cast on 82 (88, 94, 100) sts.

Beg chart 1

Row 1 (RS) Beg with st 4 (1, 2, 4) work to st 12, work sts 4 to 12 (9-st rep) 8 (8, 9, 10) times, end with st 13 (16, 14, 13). Cont in pat as established until piece measures 5½ (6, 6¼, 6¾)"/14 (15, 16, 17)cm from beg, end with a WS row.

Armhole shaping

Bind off 3 sts at beg of next 2 rows, 2 sts at beg of next 4 rows, dec 1 st each side every other row once—66 (72, 78, 84) sts.
Work even until armhole measures 4¾ (5, 5½, 6)"/12 (13, 14, 15)cm. Bind off all sts.

LEFT FRONT

Cast on 70 (73, 76, 79) sts.

Beg chart 1

Row 1 (RS) Beg with st 4 (1, 2, 4) work to st 12, work sts 4 to 12 (9-st rep) 6 (6, 7, 7) times, work sts 4 to 10 (10, 5, 10). Cont in pat as established until same length as back to armhole.
Work armhole decs at beg of RS rows as for back—62 (65, 68, 71) sts.
Work even until piece measures 7 (7½, 7¾, 8¼)"/18 (19, 20, 21)cm from beg, end with a RS row.

Neck shaping

Next row (WS) Bind off 9 (10, 11, 12) sts (neck edge), work to end. Cont to bind off from neck edge 3 sts 3 times, 2 sts 10 times, 1 st 4 (5, 6, 7) times. Work even until same length as back. Bind off rem 20 (21, 22, 23) sts for shoulder.

RIGHT FRONT

Work to correspond to left front, reversing all shaping and work chart 1 as foll:
Row 1 (RS) Beg with st 7 (7, 11, 7) work to st 12, work sts 4 to 12 (9-st rep) 7 (7, 8, 8) times, end with st 13 (16, 14, 13).

SLEEVES

Cast on 38 (40, 44, 46) sts.

Beg chart 2

Row 1 (RS) Beg with st 3 (2, 9, 8) work to st 12, work sts 4 to 12 (9-st rep) 3 (3, 4, 5) times, end with st 13 (14, 16, 8).

TINY
treasures

Cont in pat as established, inc I st each side (working inc sts into chart pat) every 4th row 11 (13, 18, 19) times, every other row 7 (7, 3, 4) times—74 (80, 86, 92) sts.

Work even until piece measures 6¼ (7, 8, 8½)"/16 (18, 20.5, 22)cm from beg, end with a WS row.

Cap shaping

Bind off 7 sts at beg of next 2 rows, 5 sts at beg of next 2 rows, 4 sts at beg of next 4 rows, 6 sts at beg of next 4 rows. Bind off rem 10 (16, 22, 28) sts.

FINISHING

Block pieces to measurements. Sew shoulder seams. Set in sleeves. Sew side and sleeve seams.

Picot edging

With RS facing and crochet hook, work around outside edge of jacket as foll:

Rnd I Work sc evenly around, so that you have a multiple of 4 sts.

Rnd 2 *Sc in each of next 3 sc, ch 3, sl st in first ch, skip I sc; rep from * around. Fasten off. Work edging in same way around lower edge of sleeves. Embroider flowers using lazy daisy st on fronts and back (see photo for placement). Cut ribbon into 3 equal lengths and attach to fronts for closures (see photo).

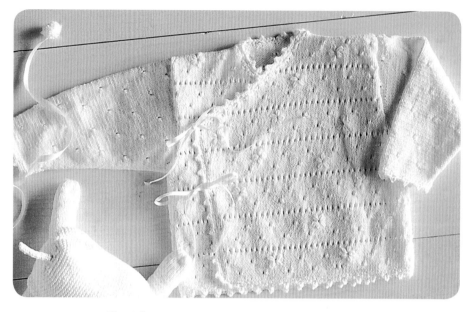

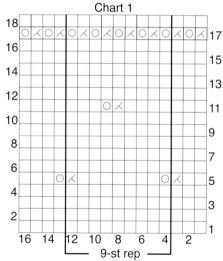

Chart 1

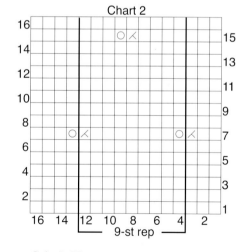

Chart 2

Stitch Key

☐ K on RS, p on WS   ⧄ K2tog

○ Yo

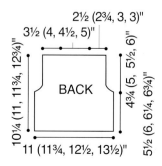

2½ (2¾, 3, 3)"
3½ (4, 4½, 5)"

BACK

10¼ (11, 11¾, 12¾)"

11 (11¾, 12½, 13½)"

4¾ (5, 5½, 6)"

5½ (6, 6¼, 6¾)"

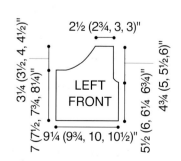

2½ (2¾, 3, 3)"

LEFT FRONT

3¼ (3½, 4, 4½)"

7 (7½, 7¾, 8¼)"

9¼ (9¾, 10, 10½)"

4¾ (5, 5½, 6)"

5½ (6, 6¼, 6¾)"

10 (10½, 11½, 12¼)"

1"

SLEEVE

5 (5½, 5¾, 6)"

6¼ (7, 8, 8½)"

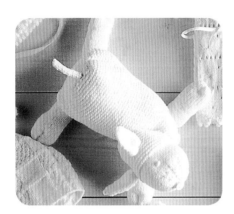

MATERIALS

Yarn 1
Any fingering weight cotton yarn,
• 1¾oz/50g, 200yd/190m in white

Needles
• One set (4) size 2 (2.5mm) double-pointed needles (dpns)

Notions
• Size B/1 (2mm) crochet hook
• Stitch marker, stuffing and one small button for nose

Lamb

GAUGE
30 sts and 40 rows to 4"/10cm over St st using size 2 (2.5mm) needles.
Take time to check your gauge.

TOP OF BODY
Cast on 22 sts. Work in garter st for 76 rows. Inc 1 st each side as foll: every 3rd row 23 times—68 sts.
Bind off 2 sts at beg of next 2 rows, dec 1 st each side every other row twice. Bind off rem 60 sts.

BOTTOM OF BODY
Cast on 14 sts. Work in St st for 114 rows. Inc 1 st each side every 14th row

twice, every 8th row 4 times—26 sts. Dec 1 st each side every 8th row 4 times, every 4th row 4 times. Bind off rem 10 sts.

PAWS
(make 4)
With dpns, cast on 21 sts. Divide sts evenly over 3 needles. Join, taking care not to twist sts. Place marker for end of rnd and sl marker every rnd. Work in St st (k every rnd) for 34 rnds. Cut yarn. Draw through sts and pull tog tightly and secure. Stuff.

HEAD
With dpns, cast on 50 sts. Divide sts and join as before. Work in rnds of garter st (k 1 rnd, p 1 rnd) for 34 rnds. Work in St st for 17 rnds. [Dec 10 sts evenly on next rnd. K 1 rnd] 4 times—10 sts. Cut yarn. Draw through sts and pull tog tightly and secure. Stuff.

EARS
(make 4)
Cast on 16 sts and work in St st for 4 rows.
Next (dec) row (RS) K1, SKP, k to last 3 sts, k2tog, k1. Rep dec row every 4th row 3 times more, then every other row twice—4 sts. Cut yarn. Draw through sts and pull tog tightly and secure. With WS of two ears tog, sew side seams.

FINISHING
Sew top and bottom of body tog, leaving a small opening. Stuff and sew opening closed. Embroider eyes on face with French knots. Sew on button for nose. Sew on legs and head. Sew on ears, gathering slightly at lower edge.

TAIL
With crochet hook, ch 2"/5cm. Sc in each ch. Fasten off and attach to lamb.

MATERIALS

Yarn 1
Any fingering weight cotton yarn
• 3½oz/100g, 390yd/360m
(3½oz/100g, 390yd/360m;
3½oz/100g, 390yd/360m;
5¼oz/150g, 590yd/540m) in white

Needles
• One pair each sizes 2 and 3 (2.5 and 3mm) needles *or size to obtain gauge*

Notions
• 1½yd/1.6m satin ribbon, ¼"/6mm wide

Undershirt

SIZES
Sized for Newborn, 6, 12, 18 months. Shown in size Newborn.

MEASUREMENTS
Chest 19 (21, 22½, 24)"/48 (53, 57, 61)cm
Length 12½ (13½, 14, 15)"/31.5 (34.5, 35.5, 38)cm

GAUGE
31 sts and 44 rows to 4"/10cm over chart pat using larger needles.
Take time to check your gauge.

NOTES
1 Be sure that there is always a yo to compensate for each dec in every row to keep st count the same. If there is not, then omit the yo or dec and work in St st.
2 K first and last st of every row for selvage st.

BACK
With smaller needles, cast on 75 (81, 87, 93) sts. Work in St st for 1¼"/3cm.

TINY
treasures

Eyelet turning row (RS) K1, *k2tog, yo; rep from * to last 2 sts, k2.
Work in St st for 1¼"/3cm more. Change to larger needles.

Beg chart
Row 1 (RS) K1 (selvage st), beg with st 4 (1, 5, 2) work to st 18, work sts 5 to 18 (14-st rep) 4 (4, 5, 5) times, end with st 20 (23, 19, 22). Cont in pat as established until piece measures 6½ (7, 7½, 8)"/16.5 (18, 19, 20.5)cm above eyelet row, end with a WS row.

Armhole shaping
Bind off 3 sts at beg of next 2 rows, 2 sts at beg of next 2 rows, dec 1 st each side every other row 4 times—57 (63, 69, 75) sts.
Work even until armhole measures 4 (4½, 4¼, 5)"/10 (11.5, 11.5, 12.5)cm.

Neck shaping
Next row (RS) Work 16 sts, join 2nd ball of yarn and bind off center 25 (31, 37, 43) sts, work to end. Working both sides at once, bind off from each neck edge 3 sts once, 2 sts twice, 1 st 3 times, 2 sts 3 times. With RS facing and smaller needles, pick up and k sts evenly around

neck edge. Work in St st for 3 rows. Work eyelet turning row as for back. Work in St st for 3 more rows. Bind off. Fold band in half to WS and sew in place.

FRONT
Work as for back until armhole measures 3 (3½, 3½, 4)"/7.5 (9, 9, 10)cm.

NECK SHAPING
Next row (RS) Work 24 sts, join 2nd ball of yarn and bind off center 9 (15, 21, 27) sts, work to end. Working both sides at once, bind off from each neck edge 3 sts once, 2 sts twice, 1 st 7 times, 2 sts 5 times. Work eyelet edging around neck as of back.

FINISHING
Overlap back 2"/5cm over the front and sew in place. Work eyelet edging around each armhole as for neck. Weave ribbon through eyelet row at lower edge of body and tie sides (see photo).

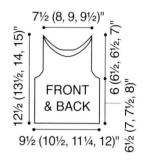

Stitch Key

- ☐ K on RS, p on WS
- ─ P on RS, k on WS
- ○ Yo
- ╱ K2tog
- ∨ K2tog tbl

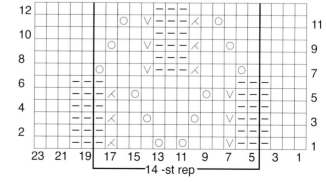

GAUGE

32 sts and 40 rows to 4"/10cm over chart pat using larger needles.
Take time to check your gauge.

K2, P2 RIB

(over any number of sts)
Row 1 (RS) *K2, p2; rep from * to end.
Row 2 K the knit sts and p the purl sts.
Rep row 2 for k2, p2 rib.

BACK

With smaller needles, cast on 80 (86, 92, 98) sts. Work in k2, p2 rib for 4 rows. Change to larger needles.

Beg chart

Row 1 (RS) Beg with st 21 (18, 3, 1) work to st 22, work sts 1 to 22 four times, end with st 12 (15, 6, 10). Cont in pat as established until piece measures 5½ (6, 6½, 7)"/14 (15.5, 16.5, 17.5)cm from beg, end with a WS row.

Armhole shaping

Bind off 2 sts at beg of next 4 rows, dec 1 st each side every other row 3 times—66 (72, 78, 84) sts. Work even until armhole measures 4¾ (5, 5½, 6)"/12 (13, 14, 15)cm. Bind off all sts.

LEFT FRONT

With smaller needles, cast on 39 (42, 45, 48) sts. Work in k2, p2 rib for 4 rows. Change to larger needles.

Beg chart

Row 1 (RS) Beg with 21 (18, 3, 1) work to st 22, work sts 1 to 22 twice, end with st 15 (15, 3, 4).
Cont in pat as established until same length as back to armhole. Work armhole decs at beg of RS rows as for back—32 (35, 38, 41) sts. Work even

until piece measures 8¾ (9½, 10½, 11½)"/22 (24.5, 26.5, 29)cm from beg, end with a RS row.

Neck shaping

Next row (WS) Bind off 3 (4, 5, 6) sts (neck edge), work to end. Cont to bind off from neck edge 2 sts 3 times, 1 st 3 times. Work even until same length as back. Bind off rem 20 (22, 24, 26) sts for shoulder.

RIGHT FRONT

Work to correspond to left front, reversing all shaping and work chart as foll:
Row 1 (RS) Beg with st 18 (18, 6, 7) work to st 22, work sts 1 to 22 twice, end with st 12 (15, 6, 10).

SLEEVES

With smaller needles, cast on 40 (42, 44, 46) sts. Work in k2, p2 rib for 4 rows. Change to larger needles.

Beg chart

Row 1 (RS) Beg with st 19 (18, 17, 16) work to st 22, work sts 1 to 22 twice, end with st 14 (15, 16, 17).
Cont in pat as established, inc 1 st each side (working inc sts into chart pat) every other row 11 (12, 9, 11) times, every 4th row 7 (8, 12, 12) times—76 (82, 86, 92) sts. Work even until piece measures 6½ (7, 8, 8½)"/16.5 (17.5, 20.5, 21.5)cm from beg, end with a WS row.

Cap shaping

Bind off 2 sts at beg of next 2 rows, 3 sts at beg of next 2 rows, 4 sts at beg of next 4 rows, 5 sts at beg of next 2 rows, 6 sts at beg of next 2 rows. Bind off rem 28 (34, 38, 44) sts.

HOOD

With larger needles, cast on 120 (124, 128, 132) sts.

MATERIALS

Yarn 1

Any fingering weight cotton yarn
• 5¼oz/150g, 590yd/540m (7oz/200g, 780yd/720m; 8¾oz/250g, 980yd/900m; 10½oz/300g, 1170yd/1070m) in white

Needles

• One pair each size 2 and 3 (2.5 and 3mm) needles *or size to obtain gauge*
• One size 2 (2.5mm) circular needle, 24"/60cm long

Notions

• Five ½"/13mm buttons

Hooded cardigan

SIZES

Sized for Newborn, 6, 12, 18 months. Shown in size Newborn.

MEASUREMENTS

Chest (buttoned) 20 (21¾, 23, 24¾)"/50.5 (55.5, 58.5, 63)cm
Length 10¼ (11, 12, 13)"/26 (28.5, 30.5, 33)cm
Upper arm 9½ (10¼, 10¾, 11½)"/24 (26, 27.5, 29)cm

TINY
treasures

Beg chart

Row 1 (RS) Beg with st 1 (21, 19, 17) work to st 22, work sts 1 to 22 for 5 (6, 6, 6) times, end with st 10 (12, 14, 16). Cont in pat as established until piece measures 2 (2¼, 2½, 2¾)"/5 (5.5, 6.5, 7) cm from beg.

Top shaping

Dec 1 st each side every other row 31 times, bind off 2 sts at beg of next 20 (22, 24, 26) rows. Work even until piece measures 9 (9½, 10, 10½)"/23 (24, 25.5, 26.5)cm from beg. Bind off rem 18 sts.

FINISHING

Block pieces to measurements. Sew shoulder seams. Using hood diagram as guide, sew hood around neck as foll: sew from A to B from front neck edge to shoulder; from B to C from shoulder to center back neck. Sew back hood seam from C to D.

Ribbed edge

With RS facing and circular needle, pick up and k 78 (86, 94, 104) sts along right front edge, 136 (140, 144, 148) sts along outside edge of hood and 78 (86, 94, 104) sts along left front edge—292 (312, 332, 356) sts.

Work in k2, p2 rib for 1 row. Place markers on left front band for 5 buttonholes, the first one at ½"/1.5cm from lower edge, the last one just below neck shaping, and three other spaced evenly between. Work buttonhole on next row at markers as foll: bind off 1 st. On foll row, cast on 1 st. Rib 1 row even. Bind off in rib.

Set in sleeves. Sew side and sleeve seams. Make a tassel and sew to point of hood. ■

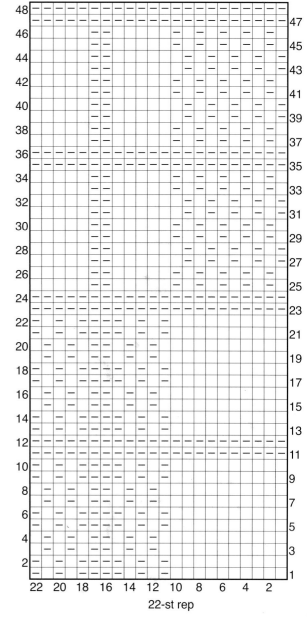

22-st rep

Stitch Key
☐ K on RS, p on WS
— P on RS, k on WS

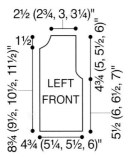
LEFT FRONT

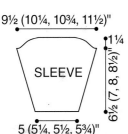
SLEEVE

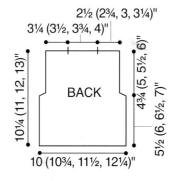
BACK

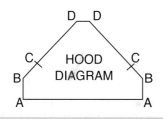
HOOD DIAGRAM